Navigating the Crisis

A Strategy to Move From the Wilderness to Success

By
Greg Brown

Navigating the Crisis

A Strategy to Move From the Wilderness to Success

Published by:
Intermedia Publishing Group
P.O. Box 1825
Peoria, Arizona 85382
www.intermediapub.com

ISBN # 978-0-9820458-6-2

TABLE OF CONTENTS

SPECIAL RECOGNITION

I would like to give special thanks to Jackie Martinez, Philip Brown and Dawn Brown for their help in editing this book. I would also like to extend my thanks to all the Skyway family who have encouraged and supported me in writing my first book. Finally and above all, I give thanks to my Savior Jesus Christ who gives me the creativity to share inspiring thoughts with all of you.

Greg Brown

ACKNOWLEDGMENT

On January 14th, just seven days before this book was to be given to the publisher, we were having our Wednesday morning prayer time at the church. At the close of the meeting Greg mentioned to the group of 60 or so intercessors that we, Greg and I, needed to make a payment to cover our initial publishing expenses. As this is a book about the supply of God, and we know that this is not the time to be increasing debt or trusting in the old debt system, it did not seem right to pull out a credit card or take an advance on our 2nd mortgage. Adding to our debt would be doing more of the same old thing and at this point in our Christian walk that seemed to be hypocritical. He asked the group to pray for us and one of our dear friends cried out, "I have a thousand dollars that I can donate." Suddenly, several people came forward with cash and started putting it in Greg's hands. Then, just as suddenly, people started praying and prophesying over us and the book. By the time the meeting was over we had over eighty percent of our initial expenses laid at our feet in cash and checks, and an expectation of the remainder of the payment to be taken care of within the week. However, for God's people that was just the starting point. Our faithful intercessors and friends wanted us to allow the congregation at our Saturday night and Sunday morning services to participate in the giving, and the reaping of rewards that comes with sowing into us and into this miracle book. Therefore, we let the need be known at the services and we were blessed by our church family with enough funds to complete this project. We are going into print with the initial 5,000 copies completely paid in full. This outpouring of love and generosity fulfilled the prophesies that the entire need would be met before going to print. And, Praise God, our credit card will remain untapped!

Some of the words that came forth in the prayer meeting are as follows: Because Greg humbled himself in front of this group, it will not fall to him to pay for this book, but that God will provide for its publishing. The money that was set at our feet, this day was appropriate in that this is a first book, not the only book from Greg or from this congregation. This is a book that will be a breakthrough for finances in the kingdom and for us. We will reach nations and will break the poverty mentality off of the body.

The Lord recently gave me a prophetic word; the following is an excerpt from that word. God is saying, now is the time. Step up and receive. "A reckoning is coming-a reckoning is coming. Be prepared to receive all that is in store for you and the church. I have an anointing for you-for the congregation. You cannot stop it-it will not be stopped. Open the floodgates; the flood is coming and it cannot be contained." My belief is that as the people of Skyway have invested in us, the spirit of poverty is being broken off of our church and our congregational family. Now is the time to unite with the vision of God and get planted. Get planted and let your roots grow deeply. It is not the time to wander. It is not the time to live a life unto your own devices. Unite, unite, unite with a body of believers and be a part of a root structure that will prosper not only your soul, but your relationships and your finances. The flood is coming; it will not be stopped. Are you ready for the flood!

As Pastor Nick Hill stated so wonderfully; "Pastor Greg, you once told me that you believed in me; this word healed a broken man. I want you to know that I believe in you too." This belief in each other for the transformation of lives, finances and society is the cornerstone of this book. Thank you Skyway for believing in us. We sure believe in you.

Be blessed as you read this book and may you prosper as your soul prospers.

Pastor Dawn Brown

FOREWORD

This is no time to be a lackadaisical Christian!

For several years now the church has been in a season of change it has not known since the Protestant Reformation of the 16th Century. This is such a radical change that it might even surpass the changes of the Reformation itself! However, God is not bringing just one change, but a whole progression of changes, each one building on the changes of the past.

That is why you and I cannot be lackadaisical if we want to fulfill the destiny that God has scoped out for our lives. We must be open to the new things that God is doing and allow change to become part of our lifestyle. To use biblical language, God is currently pouring out large quantities of new wine and we must be involved in new wineskins to receive that new wine. The old wineskins that have given us peace and comfort with the status quo must be discarded. The future will be a time of blessing and prosperity that we have never before experienced!

But the question, of course, is how do we do it? We may agree that we want to move into God's new seasons, but let's be real—what practical steps can we take to bring ourselves and our families into their God-designed destinies?

Not surprisingly, along with the new wine, God has been raising up a strong band of leaders with the assignment of forming new wineskins and of guiding believers through these multiple changes. One of them is Greg Brown. As senior pastor of Skyway Church of the West Valley in the Phoenix area, he is in touch with the people of God. That is how he knows your dreams, your challenges, and your hopes. He had you in mind as he wrote *Navigating the Crisis*. This book will bring your life and the lives of those you love to an entirely new level.

But Greg has a further assignment from God. Not only is he a pastor, but he is also an apostle. He is an active member of the International Coalition of Apostles. He is connected with hundreds of other recognized apostles. This is how he hears so accurately what the Spirit is saying to the churches. This is why he can keep track of the incredible changes that God is bringing to the body of Christ. God's usual pattern is to reveal his plans to apostles properly aligned with prophets, and Greg Brown is one of them.

Put all this together and you can see why Greg is equipped to write a book like *Navigating the Crisis*. Back to the question: I want to move into God's new seasons—how do I do it? This book is your answer. Read it with expectation. Read it with hope. Allow God to speak. It will be your road map into the future!

C. Peter Wagner, Presiding Apostle
International Coalition of Apostles

INTRODUCTION

On January 15, 2009 US Airways flight 1549 from New York to North Carolina suffered the loss of both engines within three minutes of taking off. The plane started to descend without power towards the Manhattan skyline. In 2001 we all remember the airplanes with names representing our country flying purposefully into the World Trade Center. Those aircrafts marked the beginning of the change in America we will never forget. To those watching the aircraft drifting from the sky they must have began to expect the worst. Once again a tragedy was unfolding in front of their eyes only a few blocks from the World Trade Center site.

This time the outcome was markedly different. The pilot Captain Chesley B. Sullenberger was at the helm and he was trained to save life not take it. He was a man of honor and courage; the type of person that we have not read much about in our media for the past several years. On this day Captain Sullenberger navigated the aircraft around the skyscrapers and landed it safely in the Hudson River. The people on the bank watching had been calling 911 emergency and the ferry boats were racing to the very site of the crash landing. The frigid waters of the Hudson were quickly entering the aircraft as people began to walk out onto the wings. The water was so cold that people could have died from hypothermia within two minutes. Miraculously all one hundred and fifty five passengers were rescued. Captain Sullenberger was the last to exit the aircraft after personally walking through the cabin two times to ensure all the passengers had been safely evacuated.

The news of this miraculous landing captured the headlines in cities around the world. A near catastrophe was avoided. Not because of chance or luck; but because someone was prepared for the worst and knew how to navigate the crisis and deliver passengers out of the crisis into safety. Captain Sullenberger lived his life preparing for a moment. When that moment came he was able to deliver. These headlines show us that the world is looking for hope.

Remember flight 1549 because it now stands as a prophetic sign of the hope God has declared over us for the future that is to come. The flight that appeared doomed was rescued because there was someone ready for the crisis and not afraid to take the risk of landing the aircraft in a river. God has a river for you to land safely in. He is preparing a group of people that will work in unity and purpose to save lives and you can become a part of this group. We serve the Lord who saves life! There is hope in the future for all.

There is a miracle in this book. As you begin to read, faith is going to be released into your life in a new way. You are reading this book by a choice and God is choosing to bless you. You are going to get principles into your heart that are going to transform your life. Something is going to happen and it is going to be good. I am glad you are reading this. I really am. Those of you who know me personally are aware of all the miracles God has been doing since March 30, 2008. I am talking about extraordinary miracles; I have had the privilege of being around while the Father is doing them. It is really awesome to be in His manifest presence and have someone come in and join me, the next thing you know God has released a miracle to them. I feel that same feeling right now. You are about to enter into God's manifest presence with me and He is going to work a miracle in your life. Something is already starting to be imparted. This is really strange to write but I know it is happening so I am writing it down by faith. I have read this statement a few times over and over and I can feel the presence of God being released. You may need to do this a few times also. Thank you for joining me. This is going to be fun!

On November 13-15, 2008 we hosted a Global Harvest Conference at Skyway Church. The name of it was, *Opening the Gates of Supply*. As each speaker came forward to speak the revelation continued to become more powerful. I need to introduce those speakers to you because they are the inspiration for the writings in this book.

I want to start with Dr. C. Peter Wagner. Everyone just calls him Peter. He is one of the finest men you will ever meet. He is brilliant, funny and able to stay in time with the current things that God is doing. This is remarkable. Peter released key revelation about the spirit of poverty in the church and how it is holding back the wealth that we need in this hour. He laid a remarkable foundation to understand how to break the spirit of poverty.

The next speaker was Chuck Pierce. Chuck is remarkable seeing the timing of events before they come to pass. He understands the seasons of God which is critical in moving forward in our day. He has insights about the next three years that are so very important for us to grasp. I spent the next month studying what he said and seeking God for proper biblical and practical application for myself and those I can help apply what the Lord is speaking to the church. Everyone needs to hear what Chuck Pierce is saying!

Dutch Sheets was the third speaker. Dutch brings a strong scriptural foundation to the prophetic words being spoken. He takes the scriptures and explains them in a way that is so precise and thorough. He opened up Deuteronomy 8:18 and it came alive for us. I have an entire chapter discussing this in the book. Dutch is providing passionate leadership to see the church reformed in purpose and conduct.

Lance Wallnau was the fourth speaker. Lance is brilliant. He has a revelation about the mission of the church for this hour that is life changing. Everything he says about the Seven Mountains of culture is so relevant to our time. Everyone needs to hear his seminars! He gave us the purpose for the transfer of wealth.

Pat Francis was the final speaker. She is filled with dignity, grace and great power. She gave teachings about spiritual warfare that filled us with faith. There is an authority in this woman of God that clears the demons out of the room. She releases an anointing for victory in everyone's life. She laid the foundation of the battle we must embrace.

As soon as the conference was over this team was going to another city to teach on a different subject. When they were finished I knew I couldn't just put my notes on a shelf and go on. The more I meditated upon what was said; God continued to pour additional insights into me creating a strong word that needed to be expressed. I was left with a feeling of purpose. I had to take what I learned and craft it with the word of God in such a way to help people move from crisis to purpose. This is what was laid out before me. It was a road map that I could see when all of this information was put together. The concept continued to grow until I felt this book was alive inside of me. I spoke with Peter the next month and he smiled and said, "Great! Take what we said and put it in your words and write the book!" So I did! Now it is here, I want to give honor to all of these special people who have poured the word of God into me. Now I am going to share my thoughts that God has fashioned in me with you.

The timing of the book deals with the next three years but the principles are biblical and timeless. God will always be moving people from crisis to purpose just like He has in the past. If you are reading this book more than three years after it is originally printed it will still bring a miracle into your life.

In these pages I release the process that moves people from crisis into a place of purpose and destiny. God is working in this current wilderness season. He is judging the spirit of mammon. He is moving and reforming everyone; including the church! The church is shifting from Moses the shepherd to Joshua the General; the key elements of this shift are tied to the modern day apostles, prophets and intercessors moving in alignment with His manifest presence and glory. He is preparing His people to know their assignment in the earth and to have the resources for harvest. This difficult season must be embraced with faith, not hesitation. We are going somewhere new and it is better than where we have been. In the next three years we can see a victorious move of God taking place in all seven mountains of culture. This move will include all the people of God not a select few. As the church begins to make disciples of all nations we will begin breaking the spirit of poverty and releasing the transfer of wealth. This is the time to emerge as Christ's triumphant reserve.

Chapter 1

Understanding the Future

Entering 5769 the Year of 2009

The Hebrew year of 5769 began in September of 2008. Everything that was stable began to go into crisis about this time. It was as if everything we had known as the normal standards of the financial world began to crumble before our eyes. What started as the United States' problem quickly became a world problem. By October the unthinkable bail outs became a reality. Millions of jobs had been lost and private home values had plunged. The failures of labor and monetary institutions left everyone in a state of shock and fear. All of this change and more seemed to come upon the nation and the world suddenly. How could anyone have known what was going to happen? How will anyone know how to respond? Some are asking, "Is this the beginning of the end of the world?" "Are these the signs of the return of Christ?" All of which lead us to the principles of this book. How do we navigate our lives in the midst of such crisis?

Things had been going poorly before, but everything hit crisis level at the same time. Is there a correlation between the Hebrew calendar and what is taking place? Chuck Pierce teaches every year regarding what God is going to do in that year by studying the Hebrew number and giving prophetic revelation. God is giving us insights about what is taking place and strategies to make the right decisions. How often have we looked back at history and said, "If I had only known then what I know now, I would have made different choices." This is one of those moments in our history that God is letting us know what to do before history is made. This is an opportunity to look at every event going on around us in light of these revelations and ask God to give us discernment to make the right choices. This season of crisis could actually turn out to be the best season ever in our lives.

TET (the Hebrew number nine) is the year to taste and see or to discern in a new way that God is good and He will teach us to prosper in the midst of our suffering. Know and embrace

God's goodness in the midst of your suffering.
Chuck Pierce November 13, 2008

The year we are entering into is the year of "nine." Nine is the Hebrew number TET. This number has many different meanings that are pictured through the Hebrew symbol. These will affect what is going to take place in our life this year. The dynamics of this number will have more or less emphasis upon different people but the key is to look for these opportunities to come available to you.

One word picture that is revealed by the symbol for nine is that of bowing down. This is a year to learn how to submit to the King. Many people don't like the word submission because they associate it with weakness. This is not true. *Submission literally means to be able to stand against the things that are harmful because you are under the correct authority.* When you submit to God's principles for your life you will be able to stand against the temptations that would try to drag you down and harm you.

One part of submission is alignment. This is an interesting word that the Bible speaks about in the fourth chapter of Ephesians. The word is translated as "equipping" but literally it means to be properly aligned. Think about going to a chiropractor. When the doctor aligns the body properly it is healthy to function without pain. It is able to do more and work efficiently. You will see an increase in the fruit that you will bring forth from all your labor and efforts when you are properly aligned. These are some of the benefits of being aligned.

This is the time to decide with whom you will align. Who are the people that God has brought into your life to help you move forward? This is the time for teams to prosper rather than individuals. This is a season that you need to be a part of something greater than yourself. When you bring your piece of a puzzle together with the other correct pieces then the whole picture can be enjoyed by all. How do you fit with those that you are aligned with? Is it healthy for you and for them? Everyone must benefit from the relationships we are making. Win/win is better than winners and losers. Look for these types of opportunities to align with others that will bring wins into your life this year.

There may be some alliances you need to break off. They are not helping you; they are holding you back and pulling you down. These are the relationships that use guilt to keep you connected. Guilt is not being responsible. It is feeling responsible for people that refuse to take responsibility for their own lives. Some of the old alliances may have been a win/win at one time but now they are not. The space shuttle has a rocket booster that is necessary to get the shuttle out of the atmosphere. Once it has done its job it is cut loose. If it remained attached the entire shuttle would plummet back to the earth. Are there some relationships in your life that are like these rocket boosters that need to be released?

The greatest example of faith in the bible was a military man who was not Jewish. He asked for Jesus to heal his servant because he knew how authority worked. Authority opens doors that need to be opened and closes the doors that need to be closed. Jesus marveled at this man's faith and said it was the greatest He ever witnessed in all of Israel. You can have faith that when you submit to the principles of God and correctly aligned with others many good things are coming your way. It is the principle of health. When something is healthy it produces fruit and is profitable. By being correctly connected God is going to bring His provision into your life in the years to come.

Another word picture for TET reveals a womb. This is a year to bring forth what has been conceived. Something is getting ready to be birthed. Something is getting ready to come forth through you this year. Put yourself in a position to see it come to pass! The womb represents passion. What new thing do you feel a passion to embrace? You could be sensing new desires that are being put into your heart from the Lord. If you are passionate for something that is not against the laws of God, exercise your faith and pursue it!

Travail is another part of conception. This is a year of travail. This is the painful crying out that is required for something to be birthed. It is not always a pretty sight in the delivery room hours before a child comes forth. It can get loud and messy. These things are a part of the process of bringing new life into the world. The new season God is going to bring you into may often require some travail. Don't think that God makes everything easy. In fact it is usually the opposite. If

God wants something to come forth it will require great sacrifice and pain by the one who delivers. What started with passion might move into pain before it becomes a reality in this new season of your life.

Along with the womb is nurturing. This will be a year to nurture the new season of life that God is bringing you into. Nurturing requires patience and devotion. You cannot neglect something that needs to be nurtured or it will die. There will be things that come into being this year that cannot stand alone for a couple of years. A child is a real person but they need nurturing before they become a productive adult. This new season you are embracing will require a season of nurture before you start to see the fruit of your labors come to pass. Conceive, give birth, and nurture the new life God is placing in you. Your new season which is out of your wilderness is connected to all of these steps coming together.

Entering a Three Year Crisis

A crisis can be described in many different ways. It can be a situation that has reached a critical phase. Something has to happen; it can no longer stay the same. Every crisis will cause people to turn. You have to make a decree that you are going to turn for the better and not the worse.

A crisis is a critical time or state of affairs that requires a decisive change. Change was the key word in the 2008 Presidential election. Everyone wanted to vote for change because that sounded right. The reason it sounded right is because this was a word coming from heaven. Now we need to decide what type of change is going to take place. There will be a battle between evil and good to establish strongholds in the earth as change is taking place. You have to be proactive in these next three years of your life to be a part of righteous change in all the key institutions of the earth. The harvest of souls at the end of the age is connected to you becoming a part of change. Don't let change happen; be a catalyst of righteous change. Now is the time to see it come to pass.

A crisis can also be an acute attack of pain, or distress. Once again we see the pain in the modern institutions of government, economy, family, education, media and more. This type of acute pain will continue to hit throughout the first year of this three year wilderness. Each will bring ripples of uncertainty and fear into the hearts of men. Do not allow fear to become your identity. You must get your emotions under control during this span and learn to hear a word from God that will direct you to safety. You must believe that there is a healing word coming for you during this time of crisis.

If you own a business it is important to find a new mindset for your business model. Most businesses are operating out of old methods or operating structures. They contain ideas that once worked but are now failing. The bible calls them wineskins. The businesses that will succeed will have a new wineskin to hold the new ideas that are coming. The time to make a shift is very short. As soon as you have an idea, pursue it and allow God to move you into a new season. Your wineskin will allow new ideas from heaven to come into your mind. Put them to work with your faith. Don't be afraid to try new things. In fact, I would suggest that if it is not new and innovative you should be more cautious about putting old ideas in place. Old successful plans can be a foundation to build on, but new innovations will be the key to future success.

Our emotions remember decisive moments that occur in crisis. Entire generations will be affected by what has taken place in America during the time beginning with the fall of 2008. The emotional affects will even go as deep as the Trade Center attacks of 2001 as far as how our thinking will be changed. It is important to formulate victorious positive emotions during this season of crisis. Refuse to allow yourself to dwell on what is going wrong and continually talking about it. Find something that is going right and focus upon it.

God wants us in a healthy place. If we get our emotions healthy and positive during this season we will be light to those in darkness. Think about what Jesus said, "If your light becomes dark how great the darkness will be." If we cannot be positive in this hour, who can be? God will change your emotional state if you start checking bad emotions at the gate each time they try to enter in. As I have been writing this material I have entered into a different place of faith and trust in God. It is hard for me to get focused on what is wrong. I see the great potential of good that is going to come to us. Unrighteousness is going to be uprooted and removed at this time. Wealth and supply will come to the righteous in this new season. America is not going to sink, someone is going to swim. Declare that you are going to swim in God's success in this new season!

The good news in the midst of this crisis is none of this has taken God by surprise. In fact most of this was spoken about by modern day prophets before the events occurred. God wants us to know that He is judging the spirit of mammon that has gained control of the world as we know it. Those that want to hold onto this spirit will fall; those that distance themselves will prosper. This is a season of crisis to bring about the necessary changes to prepare the earth for a harvest of souls. Jesus will come back triumphantly one day but this is a time for the righteous to shine and bring others to worship God because of their good deeds. Jesus has more for the church to accomplish before He returns and the current season of crisis is a time for the people of God to become courageous and soar.

God is giving us a blue print from heaven or a map to navigate the paths of righteousness. This is a time for everyone to live a holy life and be filled with the fear of the Lord. Judgment is at hand. The earthly judgments we are now starting to incur are truly the mercy of God to give us an opportunity to separate ourselves from the demonic methods of life that are ensnaring mankind and taking him captive to slavery. Slavery to debt, sin, depression and disease are all wrapped in the tentacles that God wants to free us from. Some of these tentacles are so familiar we have not even recognized they are connected to sin; let alone our destruction. We must not view this season as a time to go back to the *good old days*. This is not a time to mourn our losses that have been tied to the old structures.

This is a time to move forward with a clear vision of our future. God is always working with people and revealing His plans to those who will follow Him. When reading the bible we see examples from both the Old and New Testaments that reveal God's strategies for mankind to prosper and benefit by following His plans during times of crisis. In the Old Testament, Genesis chapter forty-one, Joseph was given a strategy to save the known world through the nation of Egypt with his understanding of a coming famine. Agabus spoke of a coming world wide famine in the eleventh chapter of Acts. Some might ask, "Why doesn't God prevent the crisis?" This might be a good question but a better insight is to know that He works through the crisis and provides strategies to be victorious rather than changing the events on earth. Historically this is the way that God has operated in the past and it is still a true way for God to work with us today. This book reveals God's strategies to be successful during a time of crisis. In specific it reveals plans to navigate the current and coming times of crisis during the next few years.

It seems that every institution is changing in form or operation. This includes every type of industry that employs people and generates wealth. In times past an individual industry or nation could be undergoing change. Now we see every nation and all the sectors of society dealing with change. God is still involved with us. He has not left us alone to solve these problems. He wants us to engage Him as we go through the change process. Those that learn how to do this will see strategies that create breakthroughs in the future. Those that try to continue to do what used to work will find the old ideas just don't work any more.

Embracing the Wilderness

Tell my people they are heading into a three year wilderness season. You have been thrust into an uncharted territory where we must be spoken to in this hour if we are going to make it through and into a new level of blessing.

Chuck D. Pierce

When we talk about wilderness experiences most people want to avoid them. They are not fun, but they are essential. The wilderness is actually a regular part of God's process in moving us from one season to another. There is a wilderness in between. When you read the bible about great people their lives are marked by different seasons. The same is true for every person alive; when one season ends there is a transition time before the next season. This transition is what we know as the wilderness.

The world as we know it is now in a wilderness season. People are looking at things differently than they did one to three years ago. Things they believed back then might not apply or work now. Everyone is looking for a new direction to follow. We can say they are looking for a word. Make sure that the word you are going to get comes from God!

The wilderness is where we hear a clear word from God. It is not a word that we have heard from someone else, it is where we know that we know that God has spoken to us. The amount of time you spend in your wilderness is dependant upon your ability to hear from God and act upon what you hear. The word from the Lord will direct you, give you stability and trust. Something happens when you know that God has spoken to you. Many people think that only preachers can hear from God. This type of thinking is about to change! Get busy worshipping God and praying. He will speak to you. Jesus said that everyone that belongs to Him can hear His voice. If you are one of His, start listening for your wilderness word.

The wilderness is also where we learn to trust God. Jesus, Moses, David, and Paul all had seasons in the wilderness before they demonstrated public success and victory. They were not made by the success of the new season. They were already a success by learning to rely upon God in the hidden places of trials. God has a group of people that are going through their trials right now. They will emerge triumphantly from their wilderness and become leaders for others to follow in the days ahead!

Chapter 2

Step Out of the Crisis

Develop Your New Wineskin

TET is a prophetic picture of a wineskin. This is a year to form new wineskins. Jesus said that you cannot put new wine into an old wineskin because when it ferments and expands it will break the old wineskin and all the new wine will be lost. He was talking about when things change we need to have new mindsets to allow change to become a part of our life. If we look at new ideas with the old methods, we could decide there is no room for the new idea in our life. This would be a big mistake right now. Our capacity or structure to hold the new strategies of heaven must have room to expand and grow.

Now is the time to let go of the old "walls" and get out of the box. The old methods are not producing. Look at all the old institutions that have created jobs for so many years. The wine skin is old and they have to change if new productive ideas are going to come forth. Look for new ideas that are different than anything in the past to start to emerge. These ideas will bring the solutions to today's problems. The old methods will not bring these types of solutions, their time has run out and they are contributing to the problems of today. Invest your time and money in the new wineskin.

When God moves you from one place to another you go through a wilderness or neutral zone of process before you come out into your new place or position. In the wilderness you will need to find God's definition of who you are. You are going to find God's new definition of His plan or assignment for your life. This assignment is to go to one of the seven mountains of culture and start to make a difference as a part of the Apostolos of God. You are going forward to shift the existing culture with the culture of God's kingdom. The final aspect of the wilderness is worship. Who you worship or bow to on the way up the mountain will be the god that controls you.

God's word speaks a lot about the term we call the wilderness. It is literally a desert place where you find yourself alone. It is not the judgment of God that brings you into the wilderness; it is the process of God. The wilderness is essential when one season of life ends and the next season begins. It is where the old is released and the new is identified. Jesus went into the wilderness full of the Spirit but He left in the fullness of power.

One season of thirty years of process concluded with a test that took place in the wilderness. It was there that Jesus knew His identity, His assignment, and who He would worship to access His destiny. Once this was clearly established to Him and the devil, He left the wilderness and began a new life cycle or season. The new season was in the fullness of power and news about Him spread to all the regions. His ministry shifted after the wilderness concluded. This brought about the last three years of destiny that He came into the world to fulfill. Jesus knew how to victoriously emerge from the wilderness and He wants us to do the same.

Moses is another example of a person who had a wilderness season but his did not end as well. When Moses started his season of delivering the children of Israel out of the slavery of Egypt he told the Lord that he could not speak well. This restraint in his life was met by God at the time by giving him his brother Aaron to be the one who would speak. Notice that this was Moses telling God what he could not do, not what God had said Moses was unable to do. He was allowed to get away with his excuse in that particular season. God gave him an "out" but God did not say that he did not need to overcome his constraint. God would give him forty years to grow beyond his limitations and the next season for him and Israel would provide a test for him. He would be asked to speak again at the beginning of the next season. Unfortunately for Moses he failed that test and he was not allowed to enter into the season of victory in the Promise Land.

We need to learn from his experience as we move through the seasons and cycles of our life. There are things that we might say we cannot do, but God ultimately wants us to be victorious in these areas. Refusing to try the next time around could become the end of your opportunities for a different result. What defeated you one time in your past will eventually come back to you again. This could mark the beginning or your new season. Don't be afraid of it. Don't try to deal with it the same way that produced failure the previous time. Allow God to give you a new strategy and power to overcome it and see the door open for your next season.

Moses could not move into the Promise Land because he refused to embrace a new way of thinking. This could be described as his new wineskin or cycle. In an old season Moses was told to "smite the rock" and water would come out for all the children of Israel. In the beginning of the next season that would move them into the Promised Land he was told to "speak to the rock." He was told to change his ways to get water from the rock. He heard the part about getting water out of a rock, but he relied on his old method which was comfortable. God told him to use a new method for the new season. It was his test to pass out of the old and into the new. The test involved overcoming an area he should have grown through during his past forty years.

Part of what kept Moses in his old wine skin was his emotions. Moses is revealed to have a fiery temper. His first attempt to deliver his brothers out of Egypt involved him killing an Egyptian with a shovel. This led to many years of learning in the wilderness. He needed to learn how to trust God and not his strength or ability.

When Moses was told to speak to the rock, he was insecure about his speech problem and reverted to his old ways. This was an acceptable excuse in the old season or wineskin but it was no longer acceptable to pass into the new. God expected Moses to get over his old identity and embrace his new one; the one that God had intended for him all along. The testing period for Moses seemed to come out at an inopportune time in Moses' life. He was faced with a group of complaining people on one hand and God asking him to do something he was not comfortable to do on the other. Does this sound familiar to you? Embrace your new identity! Even if you have restraints, don't view them as an excuse to fail, but a reason to glorify God when you succeed.

We tend to revert back to our old ways when we are faced with a crisis. These methods may not be very successful, but at least we are familiar with them. It does not take much effort to allow the old response to flow out of us. Be careful! God uses the crisis to allow us to put what we have learned from our mistakes into action. Moses' emotions were still out of control. God had given him time to deal with that problem in his life. His refusal to leave the old and move into the new cost him the ability to see the Promise Land. He instinctively smote the rock because he was upset. He did not listen closely to God in his season of change. He heard God in the old wine skin or thinking. He did what he had done in the past. This was a fatal mistake. God wanted him to move into a new season with his emotions under control, his ears sensitive to the voice of God, and his choices in agreement with God's direction for the new day. His crisis was his test to advance. The same is true for each of us today.

In this new season of change we must guard our hearts from acting out in old ways that are not going to be accepted in this new season. We must allow God to shift our thinking so we can be successful. New wineskins are needed to allow the new wine to be poured into. This biblical analogy Jesus gave to us years ago still applies to us today. The old wineskins get hard. They cannot expand when the new wine comes in and starts to ferment.

New ideas and strategies should be poured into our hearts and minds like an outline from heaven. When the Holy Spirit begins to expand these ideas with sentences and paragraphs of clarity we must be ready to grow and expand. This growth should be in all parts of our lives, emotionally, psychologically, physically, spiritually and more.

Never refuse to grow in any part of your life. You might be saying no to your future. If you refuse to move into the strategies of a new wine skin you will become captive in a past wine skin that will fail in the new season. What used to work in the past might be a foundation to success in the future or it might be a stumbling block to the future. Simply remaining in the old methods because they are comfortable, familiar or easy is not acceptable. Declare that you have new courage to learn new ideas and strategies for your future.

Resisting change is actually an act of rebellion. God is clearly opposed to this sin. He does not get upset with us when we try and fail. God is patient as we work through our shortcomings and remain in faith. He gets very upset when we refuse to do what He asks us to do. This is rebellion and it is demonstrated by being self reliant or self willed. This is very different than being strong willed which is actually strength of character.

Make a decision that you will not be judgmental or critical of that which you do not understand. Be careful to categorize the new things you see with the perception of old experiences. Remember that God is doing a new thing. There are some people in this season that are inflexible in their thinking. They are not going to make it into the future. They think they already know what to do because of their past experience. God warned Israel to follow Him closely in a season like ours of today. He told them that they had never gone this way before. Declare that you are willing to allow God to accomplish His will in your life. Declare that you are willing to try new methods in this new season. When I say declare, I mean say it out loud with your own voice right now!

The last thing to change is going to be your emotions. This is why we cannot be led by our emotions as we are entering into our new season. Emotions are very powerful. When this season of change came into the natural world the atmosphere was charged with many toxic emotions. The airwaves were causing people to get so upset they were dividing from loved ones. Violence, murder and slander were becoming a regular part of life experience. When the natural press is filling your emotions with rage turn it off. The gospel is the good news. We need to see what God is doing, not what the devil is doing. How much time do you allow your emotions to be controlled by outside influences? You can tell by listening to your speech. Are you constantly repeating bad news? What is your facial and body language speaking? Jesus said that what flows out of us is what fills our hearts or our emotions.

We must guard our emotions. Do not become bitter that change is occurring or angry that God is doing something different. We cannot become critical of other people that are experimenting with different strategies and pathways. What are the emotions you are feeling and expressing at this time of crisis? You have to get your emotions under control of the Holy Spirit, and declare they will not keep you stranded in an old wine skin.

Once emotions shift and are properly harnessed they can become an asset. Think of how athletes or military soldiers are trained. They are singing, marching, shouting in cadence. They are training their physical bodies, minds and emotions simultaneously as a whole to have one mind and to be ready to respond in one accord in the heat of competition or battle. This strategy has worked for thousands of years because this is how God has created man to learn.

It is time for Christians to embrace this structure of learning rather than remaining in the old wine skin of Western intellectualism. Some might think that they can silently sit and contemplate a teaching regarding a topic in order to grow. They are opposed to open displays of emotion in worship or prayer as though it is an immature response to a holy God or a poor reflection upon who they are as a disciplined person. Are you currently wired to think like this? This type of learning might bring intellectual increase but we are created spirit, soul and body. Your life is not changing just because your memory storage is increasing.

God is changing this wine skin in how we learn and express our faith towards Him. He wants to change our minds, emotions and even our physical response to Him; not only as individuals but as a group. He wants us to begin to practice the Hebraic roots of corporate shouts, declarations and raising our hands in praise. When our mind, emotions and physical response are all in one accord with good news based upon biblical truth we are shifting our selves into a new cycle of spiritual insights and victory. This will produce results in the natural realms where we live. This active expression of faith needs to be released in all spheres of life, not just at the church house on Sunday morning. Engage God's word to you in your spirit, soul, and body and see the atmosphere change all around you.

Just how do we apply such an approach to every day life? It is easier than you might think. It just takes a new wine skin or an open mind to what I am saying. When you believe that you have heard a word from God to give you direction, test it to see if it fits into the guidelines of biblical acceptance and possibility. If it does, allow yourself to speak openly about the new concept to others you trust. Allow joy to be a physical part of your expression when you speak about the word in your heart. Meditate upon it or think about it continually and allow it to grow in your understanding. This activity of your body and soul will allow the concept to become stronger inside of your spirit. As your spirit gets stronger, it will start increasing your joy and your meditation. They all work together! Don't hold your new ideas in or downplay them emotionlessly when talking about them. It is time to embrace your new ideas body, soul and spirit!

Victory will ultimately be won in the mind which controls the emotions rather than allowing the negative emotions to control the mind. Make a decision to get your emotions under God's control. Learn to become spiritually aware when they are moving back into the old nature of the flesh and the demonic forces in the air around you. Wine skins are changing because God is bringing new strategies from the Holy Spirit to us. This is a crucial time to allow God to make us soft and pliable towards changes in all areas of life.

One More Time to Get it Right

In the Hebrew year of 5769 we are in the last year of the season of sixty. As we enter into the last year of the cycle we are going to have an opportunity for old things that we did not handle well in the past to come back around to get them right. Looking back over the last ten years can you see events that have shaped your life in a negative way? What if similar situations were to come back to you? Will you simply ignore them or run from them? Will you use the same emotional medications when you see them again? What if God was giving you another opportunity to be victorious this time? This is the season that things are coming back around. This is God's mercy for us to learn new methods and principles to change the foundational patterns we use to live our lives.

As this cycle closes, we need to be victorious over emotional patterns and move forward. If we don't the broken methods of behavior and belief will become entrenched as our new wine skin for the future. You do not want this to happen. When the broken patterns become the norm in our life it is difficult to hear strategies and be victorious. Everyone will move into a new wine skin or way of living. Make sure yours is not pre-wired with destructive belief systems and behaviors. The longer you stay broken the harder it is to change. These broken beliefs about yourself, God and others will be enough to keep you in the wilderness until you die. That is not God's purpose or judgment, it is the reality of what we must deal with in life.

This is the year to get it right. Things that we thought we would always have to live with will revisit us again; this time we can be ready to handle them differently. God is amazing that His grace allows us to have another opportunity to do things differently with new wisdom and guidance. It may not be the exact same situation, but the same principles will be involved. Look at those tough things that keep popping up with a new belief that God must be giving you an opportunity to learn how to handle it correctly. He is giving you new abilities. You can have a new identity by facing your old fears and approaching them differently.

Some may not be too excited to see these familiar feelings reemerge. We will be averse to having a similar situation approaching us once again, especially if the situation brought pain and suffering into our life the previous time. The key is to not allow fear to guide you. It will always bring you pain. It will lead you down a path that you do not want to stay on. In fact, the last time you faced these problems might have you on a path that the Lord is now giving you the opportunity to get free from. Leaving the old fears and bondage to regret can be a decision away. This is the mercy of God. God is giving you the moment to seize. Move into a brand new season that He has always wanted you to live in. This can be your time of getting back on the right track towards your destiny. Don't look at the past years in regret thinking you have wasted your life. They are experiences that you needed to learn. In your life, these things could not be spoken or explained; you had to live them out. Now you have; it is time to move forward.

On the other hand, when the opportunity comes back around you could refuse to move forward. The decision is yours. God will never take away your ability to make a choice. You might be living in the pain of the past. The only medication you have had is the belief system that it was not your fault and others are to blame. Living as a martyr, controlled by the decisions and actions of others will never open the door of your self imposed prison. Even if your journey was cast upon you by the actions of others it is time to forgive and move on! Something is coming back around to help you see a permanent change come into your life. Don't miss it! If you refuse to learn from your mistakes or learn from God how to change the results of your bad decisions, you are going to be entrenched in this old life style even further. This is the opportunity to get out! Break free of the defeating life styles and habits that have formed around you. They are not your friends; they don't protect you. These things are keeping you in bondage and defeat.

When you have the chance to change take it! God is going to help you this time around. Don't try to handle everything alone. Talk to Him and ask for wisdom. Pray and wait for His peace to fill your heart before you decide. Ask for help from godly people. Get the best information to make the best decision. Even if it is difficult, ask for the power to do the right thing. God can turn the worst looking situation into a blessing if you choose to do the right thing.

Even if the consequences don't appear desirable, don't underestimate what God can do. Remember, every choice that is contrary to His written principles is outside of the boundaries of His will. Experiencing God's true destiny is connected to making choices that He approves of regardless of your circumstances. Take yourself out of the circumstances and ask this question, "Does God approve of this action or choice in His written word?" By choosing things that agree with His word we will see our circumstances change over time. Declare that you are going to see new healing over the old pains of your life. Raise your voice with a shout that you are not going to be stuck with old broken foundations in your life.

Chapter 3

Step Into Your Victory

The Cycle of Victory

The season or cycle of the sixty will be completed in 5769, this year. God has chosen to reveal a strategy for victory through the cycle of the Feasts of Israel. This will allow us to apply what we learn about the feasts into a plan to be implemented in a season of crisis. Application needs to be done where God is leading you. Don't fall into the trap that you do spiritual things at church on Sunday and natural things on Monday. You need to embrace the fact that everything you do has a spiritual purpose to be fulfilled on the earth. Learning about the feast will help you move into victory.

God reveals Himself through the set Feasts of Israel. If we understand the feasts, then we can understand how to move into victory during the cycles of change we are in. We can be led properly to prosper and not have lack when we allow God to walk us through His cycles. He reveals to us the strategies we need to be at the right place at the right time and celebrate our way into prosperity!

When we study the feasts of the Lord in the Old Testament we see that they are to be perpetually observed. This means that they did not lose relevance once Jesus died on the cross and arose from the grave to be seated at the right hand of God. They have always been written in the eternal word of God for us to learn how to bring God into our journey of life that we are living. The feasts were to be observed every year by Israel in the Old Testament and we are to observe them now through Jesus Christ and the person of the Holy Spirit.

Using the analogy of the Feasts we can see that every cycle we enter into must start with Passover. We must introduce the covenant power of the Blood of Jesus into our new field as the only source of victory over all evil and unrighteousness. We must never enter a new season, or cycle without remembering to do this. This is the sin of presumption. When we start new seasons we always start with the redemptive power of the blood to open the covenant passages of success and provision. This is why Jesus gave us the Lord's Supper and commanded us to remember him.

Can you identify your new season you are entering into? It might be a new job, promotion or partnership. Are you moving into a new city or home? You might be getting married or having a new child added to your family. Have you shifted or changed your money strategies for wealth this year? All of these types of changes in a cycle or season of your life are key times to remember Christ as your Passover Lamb. Have you renewed the covenant of the Passover Blood of Jesus Christ over you in this new season? It is easy to assume that your initial step into eternal salvation was the only time to take this step. This does not mean that you are renewing your salvation; it means that you recognize the power of your salvation through the Blood of Jesus as the source of victory in this new season of your life. This is the purpose of the cup and bread of the Lord! As often as you do this, remember Him!

To practically apply Passover to your new season you should have set time to openly declare the Blood of Jesus over all that you are embarking on. Declare that the old mindsets and failures are stopped by His victory and success. You are not held back by the failures of old, you have a new beginning created for you to enter into and experience new success. Your life is hidden in Him and you will move past every obstacle into your new position to glorify Christ to those in the world around you.

The second Feast of the Lord is Pentecost. This is the second step in our journey to victory in our cycle of change. Pentecost is ultimately connected to the Holy Spirit coming to the church. Remembering Pentecost is the second step that is essential to move forward in your new season. So often we assume that the pledge of the Holy Spirit for our eternal redemption is all that there is to the person and work of the Holy Spirit. Some might believe that He simply is residing inside of us in a dormant state until one day we die and then He redeems us. Others might have a perception of the Holy Spirit through mystical experiences in a church setting that have no relevance outside the walls of a church. We must break through these past stereotypes if we are to find true success in our new season that we are entering.

We must learn to receive revelation from the Holy Spirit to navigate our new field. This means that we learn to hear the inner voice of God giving us direction for decision making in this new season of our life. Jesus Christ is the wisdom of God. Successful people have wisdom as a characteristic of their life. The people of great faith listed in Hebrews Chapter eleven had one particular element in common. They had the capacity to hear what God wanted them to do on the earth before they were able to demonstrate faith for it to actually happen. The Holy Spirit is inside of you to give you the mind of Christ. We need His mind for this time more than ever before. Declare in your prayer you can hear the voice of God's Spirit. Thank Him for speaking to you. Say that you will obey the directions He is going to give you in this new time of your life. This is a partnership and He has the majority role!

 We must rely on the power of the Spirit to overcome the enemies in our field. The bible tells us that we have an enemy that has devised specific schemes designed to defeat us in our destiny and purpose to glorify God on the earth. The bible tells us that our enemies are not sourced in the natural realm of flesh and blood and the weapons for our victory are not based in the natural realm. Our weapons are supernatural or above and beyond the natural. All of this means that we must learn how to bring the power of the Holy Spirit into our daily life. Our prayer life, which will be discussed in detail later, must have an expectation of supernatural power being released to defeat the enemy and his plans to stop you short of your divine assignment. This new season must be the time that you make a conscious effort to put the super on your natural if you plan on being victorious. We must be supernaturally empowered or anointed to be the best in our field.

The number nine is significant because it speaks about the nine gifts of the Holy Spirit. The gifts of the Spirit are to be expressed by everyone who belongs to Jesus Christ. They cannot be relegated to what we do during a church service; they are given to us to make us profitable. When we declare that the Holy Spirit can release His gifts in all aspects of our life, we become supernatural people living in a natural world. There is supposed to be something different and better about people that have the Spirit of God living in them. We need to embrace our new season with a willingness to access the supernatural abilities of God. We need these to combine with our natural talents and knowledge. To move to the top of your new field you need the

Holy Spirit to give you more than all the good things you already have in you. When you combine supernatural power with natural talents you will be unstoppable!

The number nine also speaks about the fruit of the Holy Spirit. This is a reflection of the character of God being developed in us by the Holy Spirit. Fruit is the by product of a branch that is properly attached to the tree. The life of the tree flows through the branches and the fruit is what everyone eats to find nourishment. God wants people to find His nourishment for their lives through us. Love, joy, peace, patience, goodness, kindness, gentleness, and self control are attributes we can have every day because of the Holy Spirit. Thank Him for being inside of you right now. Declare that His life will flow freely in your character as a person.

The third and final Feast of the Lord is Tabernacles. This feast is the joyful harvest of abundance and provision and was identified with great celebration. Celebration is a part of God's plan for us to move into our new place in life with victory. Somehow celebration has been robbed from many people. It has been associated with excess and abuse, or known as partying. It seems that people who mature beyond such indulgence lose their desire to celebrate. Enter into your new season with a willingness to celebrate God, life and your opportunities which are open before you. Teach those around you how to celebrate by having them join you with each success along the way. Celebration is essential to move forward and become victorious.

The Feast of Tabernacles is where we see the harvest of our efforts in being fruitful as we advance the kingdom of God. God did not command us to try to bear fruit; He said that we would bear fruit and it would remain. Every season and cycle we enter we must have faith for this season of fruitfulness to be a part of our lives, business, family and church. Survival is not our goal. Fruitful multiplication with great joy and celebration is our destiny. Have a genuine expectation for this to be the end result of your new season you are now entering. Believe that your business is going to succeed and make money. Believe that you are going to advance in your company and make others around you benefit from your participation. This benefit to others will bring a benefit to you. Harvest is not being selfish; it is a part of God's cycle of life. Every season we enter into needs to be finished off with a harvest. False humility which is really pride or fear will tell you harvest doesn't matter. Cast off these mindsets from the past that are trying to rob you of your destiny and dream. Every season has a harvest or it ends in disappointment. You are leaving disappointment and moving into purpose. Declare that you will reap a harvest in your new season. Make it a part of your purpose as you move forward.

These three Feasts of the Lord give us God's strategy for how to enter into new seasons and cycles and come out victorious. As the Lord is bringing everyone on the earth into a new season of change, we have His strategy for success. It is our responsibility to put this strategy to work as we move forward into our new seasons. Remember to start the new cycle with the power of the Blood of Jesus. Be specific about allowing the Holy Spirit to lead and guide and empower you in strategy and warfare. Expect a victorious harvest to be reaped in your new field and celebrate God's goodness before, during and after the harvest season with those with whom you are aligned. Put all three feasts into action this year as you move forward out of your crisis.

Ten Keys to Move Into Your Future

All scripture is inspired by God and is profitable for us. There are some scriptures that we need to grasp hold of to carry us through certain times in our life. Psalm thirty four is one that we need to memorize and stand on as we face this time of crisis. This is a Psalm of praise in a difficult time. The principles that are given to us for instruction will release joy and hope.

The weight of negative words, attitudes and emotions will burden us greatly in a wilderness season. Many are not aware of how negative the emotional climate in which they live is charged. It is crucial that we maintain positive and joyful emotions every day when there is a crisis. This is crucial to be victorious.

Each of the first ten verses of Psalm thirty four can be used as a declaration of victory. I have broken down the first ten verses to be ten steps you can declare each day to remain confident as you are passing through your wilderness.

Psalms 34:1-11 (NASB)

[1] I will bless the Lord at all times; His praise shall continually be in my mouth.

It is time to decide that I will bless the Lord at all times, not just when things are going my way. This is a season of exuberant praise. God is ordaining it this way to give us the joy we need to overcome the stressful emotions we are facing. Praise is our spiritual weapon of war to uproot and evict the enemy standing in our gates. We need to get all negative, complaining speech out of our mouth. Refuse to be bitter. Remember, how we praise in our gates is how we will dominate in our new season.

[2] My soul will make its boast in the Lord; The humble will hear it and rejoice.

This is the season to get our soul under control. The old season was filled with soulish indulgence. It was all about me. That season is over and this is the time to start putting God first and dealing with our flesh. When we humble our self we will be able to hear a word from God to make it out of this wilderness season. Put God first in deed, not just word.

[3] O magnify the Lord with me, And let us exalt His name together.

The old season of exalting mammon is under God's judgment. This is the time to magnify the Lord. Refuse to enter into all the negative talk about how bad things are going to be. Start talking about how God is going to deliver you and this world by the power of His kingdom. Let's exalt His name together!

[4] I sought the Lord, and He answered me, And delivered me from all my fears.

Here are three simple keys to remember. I will seek the Lord in this season for a word to direct me. When we do this God promises to answer us! God promises to deliver us from all our fears! Declare right now, I will seek the Lord for His answers and delivering power to become a part of my life!

⁵ They looked to Him and were radiant, And their faces will never be ashamed.

This is the season to look to God. When we do we will shine with His glory upon our face. You are not going to be ashamed when you fix your future upon your God.

⁶ This poor man cried, and the Lord heard him And saved him out of all his troubles.

Jesus said that there is a blessing to the poor in spirit. There is a blessing to be humble in this hour. When we humble ourselves and cry out to the Lord He promises to save us from all our troubles! Declare that God is going to deliver you out of this crisis!

⁷ The angel of the Lord encamps around those who fear Him, And rescues them.

This season is more than a time of crisis. It is also the invasion of the supernatural. Angels have an assignment to help the heirs of salvation. Decide to walk in the fear of the Lord instead of the fear of man. This will open up the windows of heaven. Embrace the supernatural in this season and you will see how God rescues you!

⁸ O taste and see that the Lord is good; How blessed is the man who takes refuge in Him!

This is the key verse of scripture for this season of crisis. God wants everyone, even those who have never known Him to taste and see that He is good. He is good to those who will take refuge in Him during this time.

⁹ O fear the Lord, you His saints; For to those who fear Him there is no want.

God is judging the world system that tries to fill our lives with fear and dread. When we learn to fear Him we will break free of this old system and God promises that we will have no lack! Declare now, I will fear the Lord and suffer no lack!

¹⁰ The young lions do lack and suffer hunger; But they who seek the Lord shall not be in want of any good thing.

This season will see many suffering. Even those who normally are strong will suffer and be hungry. This is not the fate for those who learn to seek God in this time. There might be difficulties but I am going to experience this promise. Declare that I will seek the Lord and I shall not want any good thing!

It is crucial that we meditate upon the word of God so our attitude is changed for the better. Our path will be decided by our attitude. Every negative emotion that we allow to direct us will direct us towards trouble. Every person that is following us will follow us into trouble if that is where we are headed. Use God's word as the source for developing a positive attitude.

Chapter 4

Changing Your Financial Crisis

Economic Strategies

Money is going to be a central theme in this new season. It is going to be in the middle of the news as well as private discussions. There is a reason the bible says that money answers all questions. There will be people that do not believe there is enough money to survive. Some of the old sources of wealth will dry up. This will lead to continual discussions of recessions, depression, and inflation. Don't get caught up in all of this negative talk with negative expectations. If someone tells you that sixty percent of the businesses are going to fail, declare that your business is in the other forty percent. If they say that a certain percent is going to be out of work, decree that you are in the other percent that is working. You must embrace a new economic strategy for this new season. This is essential for you to navigate out of the wilderness into God's purpose for your life. God will have enough in this season; we need to properly align with His supply.

God wants us to think about the storehouses that need to be built in this time. Every season has a place where money is stored and resources multiplied. It is time to get out of the old season of saying that debt is good. In God's economy it is a curse. Where are you putting your money? If the extent of your economic plan is to pay this month's bills before next month's bills come in, you need a new plan! This is a season to start envisioning yourself being debt free. Don't continue to buy things you cannot afford. Pay off existing debt until you are ready to start saving your money. Develop a plan to save and store now. Your plan can open the gates of supply for resources to start coming in.

God gave Joseph a strategy of storing up wealth in storehouses in the seven years of plenty so that there would be food for the entire world in the seven years of famine. This was a strategy. We are entering into a new seven year period that will have three years of crisis. The first year may be spent praying and travailing over your plan. You will give birth to new ideas that will increase in fruitfulness over the years to come. These new ideas are going to be business and employment strategies. Every sphere where people work needs to know what is changing and how to change in the right way. Refuse to be stuck in an old structure that will not allow you to prosper financially in the future. God is creating partnerships and aligning people for wealth to multiply. There will be many in crisis suffering lack but this is not God's destiny. This is the season that He is moving finances into the hands of the righteous. Declare that you are in His plan. Money will always be in the hand of someone; you just need to start putting a strategy together that God will allow money to flow your way.

Some people may not want to talk about increasing their revenue streams because it sounds ungodly. This type of thinking is very religious but it is not biblical. In every great revival recorded in biblical history God used great amounts of wealth to change the perception the known world had about Him. He had godly people put this wealth to use in ways that glorified Him. The same is going to be true in this season. Money that could be used to destroy lives and keep them in bondage can be transferred into the hands of people that will use it to save lives, improve our world conditions and care for the poor. If God gave you wealth would you be willing to put the money to work for these types of efforts? If so, you need a strategy to build wealth during the coming years.

The central theme in this hour of crisis is God's judgment upon what the bible calls Mammon. Mammon is a world system based around finances that excludes God and His principles regarding money. Money is a spiritual force that takes on the identity of the one who holds it. If it is held by a person without godly morals it can create great harm. If it is held by someone that is under God's influence it can bring great help.

Mammon will use the power of greed to cause people to destroy others and their own selves by continually trying to gain more wealth for selfish ambition. This is what God is judging in this crisis. Everyone and everything that is under the influence of Mammon will be shaken until they are free of its power. If one refuses to let go of the influence of Mammon, they will suffer great loss at this time. No one is immune from this. People at the highest levels of wealth are being dealt with regarding how they make their money and what they do with it. This judgment is God's mercy. What we suffer and learn from on earth allows us to turn to God and change before we enter into an eternal destiny.

Make a decision right now to move as far away from Mammon as possible. Mammon wants you to believe that there is not enough money around for you and others. It wants you to believe that you must hoard what comes your way because it may leave at any moment and you will still be in a state of lack. Take a moment to study and identify how many of your decisions are influenced by Mammon. When God reveals to you the ways that Mammon has affected your choices start doing the opposite to break free from its grasp on your heart and mind.

The key is to do the opposite of what it wants to make you do. Generosity is the nature of God. Being generous while you are suffering is a strategy to getting free and finding your storehouse plan. Developing a giving strategy before you gain wealth is a key part of entering into God's supply. What you are going to give will determine how much will come in! The beginning points of God's biblical strategy of generosity are as follows: the tithe, offerings, alms and first fruits offering.

The tithe or ten percent of the gross amount you receive is to be given to a storehouse that is doing the work of God and feeding you spiritually. This should be your local congregation to which you are connected. The offering is any place you see need and your heart wants to help. Alms is helping the poor or caring for members of your family. The last portion called first fruits is a powerful offering that shows your faith in God's ability to provide for you and increase your provision. It is any amount of money that you want to give *before* God blesses you or it is a set amount that represents the first and the best of what has started to create wealth in your life. You may be starting a new business venture and put in a first fruits offering when you start as an act of faith. Once it actually makes money you can give any amount of the first portion of money to God as an act of faith that it will be blessed with abundance in the future. You are giving God the first portion in faith that it will be bountiful!

Who you are connected to or aligned with will be a significant factor in your storehouse strategy. Look for people with a *kingdom of God mentality.* God is going to be advancing His kingdom not personal agendas. Kingdom people care more about promoting God than their name or brand. Some use God to advance their plans while kingdom people sacrifice their plans for the sake of growing God's kingdom. When you are giving to kingdom causes and connected to kingdom people your supply from heaven will come in. God is giving us new ideas to advance His kingdom to allow people to see Him as loving and generous. These storehouses will be filled from heaven in this season.

God has a divine storehouse plan for every person and your provision for the season of crisis is connected to your storehouse plan. How many streams of income do you currently have coming into your storehouse? Ask God to give you a strategy to increase these streams. What gifts and talents do you have? Start to pray about how these gifts and talents can be used to increase income into your life. Work with what God has given you rather than trying to make money in ways that you do not understand. Creating wealth does not have to be difficult. When we flow in the supernatural gifts and talents in places that God has ordained us to work or serve we will see finances flow into our life. Remember most of the body of Christ works outside of the local church but everyone is called to walk in the supernatural gifts. Find out of this can work in your life. God has called you to do this to give Him glory. Start asking Him for a storehouse strategy now!

In Psalm twenty three God is described as *My Shepherd.* This is an important scripture to hear in this season of building your storehouse. You must connect with God in this manner. Wake up in the morning and decree this scriptural principle over your life…

> *The Lord is My Shepherd*
> *I shall not lack or want in this season.*
> *He will allow me to rest in green pastures.*
> *These pastures are going to sustain me.*
> *He leads me by water that is going to nourish me.*
> *My soul is being restored.*
> *I am healthier now than ever before!*
> *He guides me in new paths of righteousness.*

There is a righteous success factor on my path.
God is going to show me my success factor in this hour!
My covenant with him is why I will find success!
Even when the shadow of death is all around me
I will refuse to be controlled by fear or evil.
I am comforted and directed by God's guidance and authority.
God has me feast at his table even when
my enemy tries to surround me.
I have a new anointing for this hour.
My life is overflowing with God's presence.
I have a covenant of goodness and mercy all
the days of my life; even in a crisis!
I will dwell in the house of the Lord forever!

Change your Form

Last year your field was making a shift. How do I know; because every field is shifting. This is a season of a great change or transformation for everyone. People who believe in God and those who do not are all living in the same time frame that is seeing everything being altered from one state to another. Are you ready to lead the way by embracing change or are you going to resist it and be left behind?

You have read enough by now to know that this period of time is upon us and wishing it was not will not change anything. It will only make whatever is going wrong continue to become worse because you are not being proactive. You need to believe that God has you reading this book because He wants you to be transformed in your thinking, living, and profitability!

Everyone is going through an alteration from one state to another. Can you identify how this is happening to you? This is the year for you to move into a different form or quality. You can become victorious over old ways of thinking that have previously held you back. This can be your year to face old giants in your life that you have feared in the past. This time you are going to be filled with new strategies from heaven to face them and be victorious. Most have heard the story of David and Goliath. God reveals many of His principles in this familiar story.

I would like to quickly recap the situation for modern application. God was working on a huge scale that affected everyone. The entire nation and army of Israel were powerless with fear because of a giant named Goliath. David was in a wilderness learning new skills that would be put to use in a new season. His transforming from shepherd to king began with the declaration of the prophet of God, yet everyone around him only recognized him by his past natural position. He was simply a shepherd boy to everyone else; everyone else but God.

David was in a transition season. God had already decided to change kings while Saul was king over Israel and David was an unknown shepherd boy. David spent his days in his *wilderness* acquiring the skills to protect his flock from predators like lions and bears. How would you like to spend your private life literally facing lions and bears? David's transition from shepherd to warrior began with the request of his father to take supplies to his brothers and the army of Israel.

When David submitted to the authority of his father and went forward to the battle field he was given the new insight from heaven on how to defeat the giant. (Remember this is a year of submission.) His battle plan was not a sling shot as most obviously recognize. David heard a spiritual word from heaven from his place of wilderness. This word would come to him, but it would benefit the entire nation. Our God ordained destiny will always benefit others in fulfilling God's heart for man. David heard a word from heaven that would give him the faith to face the giant no one else living in the old wine skin of thinking would do; not even the current king, Saul. David understood that the victory would not come through natural means but supernatural means. He felt that the key to victory was found in the covenant plan of God for Israel and himself. He viewed the battle as between God and the giant, not himself and the giant. He was filled with a word that no one else had. This was his strategy for the new day.

David was offered the armor of King Saul to use in his battle. Saul could not see a new weapon or strategy because he was entrenched in the old system that was powerless to face the giant problem of his day. David declined because it was not something he was going to use in the new day of battle. You cannot fight today's battles with last season's armor. You cannot trust in the strength of man to do what only God can do. David confidently told the giant that he was going to fight him in the Name of his God! Your wilderness is where you will find your word from God. When that word becomes so real to you that any giant standing in the way of God's plan gets you ready to fight, look out! You are being transformed into a different person. Do you see how this story is really a picture of how God can alter you into a new person with a new season while no one around you can even recognize anything different is going on?

David said something very powerful to the giant before he went into battle. He made a declaration that he would cut the giants head off. He was holding five stones and had no sword. The only sword around when he made that declaration was in the giant's hand. David knew that the very weapon fashioned to destroy him would be turned on his enemy to remove his authority! We give the devil too much credit and too much authority in our lives. Your crisis that seems to be a tool in the devil's hand can be turned around to be a tool in your hand to remove the demonic structures and plans against you! This word was real to David. It was not written in a book, it was written in his heart. The moment of transformation from shepherd to warrior was upon him and he seized it. In a moment of testing David allowed God's word over his life to become a reality in the way he lived his life. The word changed David into a new man rather than David trying to fit the word to work in his old way of living. If you want to become someone new, let God's word change who you are in private and public.

David's victory over the giant had some key subplots as well. His heavenly strategy for success was rooted in his love for God and the nation of Israel. He could not stand to see an enemy mocking his God or people. He was kingdom minded first and foremost. When you care more about God's kingdom than your own life you will always step up to advance the kingdom. When God's kingdom is the first thing we seek in our life, fear will never be able to stop us.

David was also told of a benefit that was offered to anyone who would destroy the giant. He would become wealthy and marry the king's daughter. David verified the benefits before he went to battle. The personal benefits were not his primary motivation but he was wise enough to accept them. When David shifted from one field or occupation to another to glorify God, he experienced increase in wealth, status, and public fame. Those who go to battle for these reasons might find shame and failure, but if we accept our challenge for the right reasons these benefits are not to be rejected as evil. They were part of God's transformation plan for David. God knew He could trust David with all of these benefits because David was living for God, not the benefits of being connected to God. This is an important principle to grasp to move out of the wilderness.

To put this in a different way; if you do not make your shift in form and quality you will not move into your next level of profitability. You cannot be rigid or you will be left in an old wineskin or way of living which does not bring you into God's prosperity for this season. This is a season of succession from one order into another. This is time for the removal and or alteration of one order to produce another order. Your ability to profit is connected to your ability to change what you are doing or how you are doing what you are doing now. It is connected to who you are working with and aligned with for the future. Your covenant with God and man will determine how your connection to heavenly supply is formed.

David aligned himself with God, God's nation, and God's new position for him. He seized the moment when it was before him. He went through the window of opportunity when it opened. All of this took place while the nation was in a crisis and everyone else thought the window of opportunity was locked shut.

Someone has to be the first to show everyone else something new is happening. You might be that person, or you might be aligned with these people. Refuse to allow the crowds paralyzed by fear to tell you how to move forward. Get your word from God and let it empower you to see yourself in a new light. Take the necessary steps to live out your new life in public. You will know when to step forward when the authority you are under sends you out. David trusted his father Jesse and he trusted his God. He loved God's kingdom and relied on the covenant to make him victorious. Declare with me that you are going to move out and be a part of the new victorious generation. Decree, my God will fight for His covenant promises to be fulfilled in my life!

Success Factors

We are entering into a revolutionary time. A revolution or a season produced by a revolution is now upon us. The very nature of a revolution is associated with a revolt or uprising against the existing authority. Every sphere of influence is experiencing change at the top. Industries are changing. You can be a part of this change for the glory of God. You can move into and represent the new authority in the future if you take the right steps now.

If you do not prepare for this in your business, or career employment, you will not be prepared for what is transpiring. In order to make the shift you need to be asking the Lord to give you insights. "How is my field shifting?" What is the revelation I need from heaven for me to prosper in my field?" Start believing that new ideas are going to come forward for you.

Jehoshaphat was a king in the bible that was in a crisis. Several strong nations conspired to join forces as one to defeat Israel. This battle was so different he knew he needed a new plan; the old way of battle was not going to work. He asked for the Lord to give him direction. When it came it brought forth a unique way to go into battle. God told him to send the people who sang praises to the Lord in front of everyone else. This included the warriors and people with natural weapons! This was one season when being in the army band was not a cushy job! He asked for a strategy and when he received it he acted upon it. His obedience to this new idea from the Lord gave them a huge victory over all the nations that had come to destroy them. When Jehoshaphat accepted and acted upon his new strategy from heaven he experienced success on earth.

Success can be defined as a favorable outcome or result. It includes the gaining of wealth, fame, rank etc. Success is the result of being correctly aligned in such a way that that everything is right, fitting, and proper. When we are aligned properly we will prosper and succeed. Think of how good your body feels when everything is in alignment as compared to the pain and difficulty you have when it is not. Proper alignment has a byproduct of good health and success! Now is the season to align.

Joshua is anther godly leader that moved successfully out of the wilderness into a new season of purpose. His purpose was connected to the purpose for all of Israel. God promised Joshua that success was his destiny if he meditated on God's word continually. His mind had to be so focused upon God's strategies he could not receive fear from his circumstances. This is a strange place to be. You know when you are there because fear cannot stop you from moving forward with the plan that has been placed into your heart. If fear is stopping you, meditate on God's written covenant word and the prophetic word He has spoken into your heart.

Meditation is not a mystical thing you do with your eyes closed and fingers held in a circle. Meditation comes from the Hebrew word picture of a cow chewing the cud. This is the process of the grass being transformed into nutrition for the cow. The grass goes from one stomach to another until it transforms into a different state. It becomes liquid nutrition which gives life to the cow. We must meditate upon all that we have been instructed to prosper and succeed in the coming years.

Meditate upon the manifestation of an expectation that you have hoped to see come to pass. Meditation will give you the power to achieve a desired outcome. It will help on your road in reaching your destination. Focusing upon the blueprint that God has given you will bring well being and fulfillment into your life.

The Lord is giving some clear ideas on how you can find success in this revolution season. Like King Jehoshaphat mentioned above, you are being given information that most have not applied before now. This is the time to put these practices to work. Someone has to be the first. Memorize this principle and it will propel you forward into your destiny.

David and Jehoshaphat both had strong worship of God in common. This is not an accident; it is a precedent. Every kingdom has a king and every king demands worship from his subjects. The gods of this world are demanding worship and adoration. They want our time, money, and thoughts. The defeated structures that are falling today have already bowed the knee to evict God from their culture. Now as they worship the fallen gods, they are falling as well.

Worship is always crucial in moving out of the wilderness and into the future. This is a season of kingdom clashes. Every "strongman" desires worship. To supplant the existing strongman that is keeping you from advancing into your destiny and dream you must have a worship strategy that is greater than his. How we worship is how we build our wine skin and get our revelation for our storehouse. How we worship in our field is how we will dominate in our field. Becoming spiritually minded in your place of occupation will bring you to a new level of success. You need to implement the following success factors to navigate through the crisis and enter into a season of harvest.

#1 *You need to rebuild your altar to make your shift successful.* Heaven must be invited to invade your field no matter what field you are in. In the past people thought that they did all the spiritual stuff on Sunday and went to work on Monday. Victory will come to those who go to their place of employment and start inviting God and all of His forces to the geographic points of business and the sphere of business they represent.

#2 *Start by designating an altar* or a place to meet with God, at your place of business. Every business should start gathering kingdom minded people to pray. This can be all the people who work for one business or gathering those from different business interests together to pray for the entire field of business.

#3 *Set a time of meeting with God* just like you would with your associates. Don't fit God into your schedule, give Him your calendar and ask Him when and where you should be gathering to meet with Him.

#4 *Pray for the company to be a blessing* to all who represent it and associate with it. The most practical thing you can do is pray for the people who work with you. Pray for the people who own the company. Pray for the vendors that work with your company. Make a strategic prayer plan to pray for everyone connected and aligned with you.

#5 *Pray for God to be glorified* by the company and its conduct. Ask God for righteousness to be released by the people and the product of the company. Pray for tangible benefits to be the byproduct of what is produced by your group. Pray for your company to be a kingdom minded company.

#6 *Incorporate praise and worship into the business.* Praising God will break the airwaves of demonic clutter and interference. The music can be very subtle or professionally used on phone lines and intercom systems. Keep the praises of God going twenty four hours a day.

#7 *Confess the power of the blood of Jesus* as the covenant strategy for your success. Jesus has made a way and He is your Lord. Your victory is based upon His victory. He wants you to succeed and has already prepared the way.

#8 *Pray for the strategies of heaven to invade your sphere of authority.* Every believer has a sphere of authority. Your authority is connected to where God has planted you. You might be the owner of the company or the receptionist. If you are planted in that field you have spiritual authority in that field. Ask God to show you how to use your authority to dislodge the powers of darkness working against you. You need to go to work with your spiritual armor on every time you leave to go to your place of employment!

#9 *Pray for the Lord to give you a blueprint* of what your change should look like. Think of it as a heavenly business plan. Your prayer time should release new energy, excitement and strategy to see godly success enter into your field!

#10 *Begin confessing, decreeing and declaring* your blueprint is an earthly reality. Don't question God once He has given you the strategy; be His voice on earth to declare His will and His kingdom to come upon the earth.

#11 *Build your field* according to the blue print from heaven with acts of obedience on earth one step at a time. Little by little you can bring a new environment and atmosphere to your field.

#12 *Refuse to fight against or resist change.* Learn to accept change so you can create a new wine skin to operate in.

#13 *Ask God to teach you how to rule* in your sphere of authority. You need to move from being a part of the field to learning how to dominate in your field. When we learn to accept change we will begin to learn to rule our sphere and this will release seeds of success and we will begin to profit.

#14 *Declare that this is a year of the fruitfulness.* This requires us to include the person and work of the Holy Spirit in our vocation.

#15 *Pray for the* nine gifts of the Spirit and the nine fruits of the Spirit to be a regular part of our lives where we work and live. You can suppress your profitability by not accepting the gifts of the Spirit. You must allow the gift of God to come alive in you to profit. You must allow the "super" to become a part of your "natural."

#16 *Pray for a new relevance in your field.* Do I have a relevant message? How will others profit from my message? These questions need to have practical answers and applications to navigate and move forward.

#17 *Pray for a strategy for others to be compelled to join or follow you in your field.* This is a season of alignment. No one is going to succeed alone. Building successful teams is crucial to experiencing success.

#18 *Pray for your success factor to enter your path.* God wants you to succeed. God is going to bring someone on your path to help you succeed and be properly aligned for prosperity.

#19 *Pray for old connection dreams that will hinder success to be removed.* Create a list of what did not come to pass and move them forward or decide which of those are now out of time and let them go. Identify the relationships that are stopping you from moving into your new season. Ask God to change them or remove them. This is a time to multiply!

#20 *Pray for a Harvest strategy.* Develop a place and strategy for harvest in your new business plan. Give birth to something this year that will create a harvest in the years to come. Refuse to give your life for something that will not be able to bring a harvest in the new season that is upon you! This is a season to multiply. Declare that you are going to see your harvest start forming now and you will gather it in the future!

God declares that He has a triumphant reserve that is forming. They are being prepared through years of trials to possess the spoils at the right time. This group is going to be called forth to lead in the next season on the earth. You need to declare that you are a part of this triumphant reserve!

Chapter 5

Changing the
Spiritual Atmosphere

The Judgment of Mammon

What is the transference of wealth? The transference of wealth that is being discussed by many prominent Christians can be defined as the *cycle of change of wealth from the unrighteous to the righteous to steward wealth. God promises to change the cycle from unrighteous to righteous.*

Chuck Pierce on November 13, 2008

The banking and credit crisis of 2008 which seemed to have been unfathomable to some actually was unavoidable when looking at the principles of God. You cannot say that the things God declares to be evil are good and get away with it forever. The spirit of Mammon created a belief system in America that said debt is good. The term, other people's money became a catch phrase for everyone to get rich quick, but eventually someone had to pay. Living as a debt based society in a time that personal savings had shrunk to an all time low caught up with everyone. This included the Federal Reserve, major lending institutions and our national congress. When the time came to hold someone accountable for the trillion dollar bailout from congress, everyone seemed to be completely surprised that the debt based system collapsed; everyone except for the Lord.

God's word is filled with principles that will last forever. The crisis that the world is in will not be solved with solutions that go against these principles. Most people have drifted so far away from a biblical righteousness they don't know where to turn when the crisis comes upon them. Those who trust in God can hear a word to direct them to success in this season of crisis. Yes, you can prosper when things are difficult. The key to success is learning to submit to the principles of God regarding wealth and finances. When we submit to God's ways, we are going to move onto the righteous paths. The promises of God connect wealth and prosperity to living a godly life.

This crisis is connected to the judgments of God. We can think of God's judgment in two ways. The first can be the natural results of cause and effect when we live outside of the boundaries He has established. In this way, we bring judgment on ourselves by the choices we make. Even if we do not know these are unrighteous choices, there is a price to pay over time.

The second aspect of the judgment of God is His mercy. The mercy of God triumphs over judgment. Understanding how this works is crucial in this hour. The judgment is the consequences for choices outside of God's established principles. God is able to bring good into our lives because we realize we are outside of His will when the pain of our choices comes upon us. This pain should cause us to cry out to God for help. When we do, He reveals to us the pathways that He has established for us to follow. When we get redirected onto His paths we can find mercy, forgiveness and a new opportunity to succeed. The judgment of God in our earthly decisions shows us that we need to submit to Him in all things. This brings prosperity into our life on earth. When we submit our eternal destination to Him as well, we will find eternal redemption which is the ultimate prosperity for man.

In this hour of crisis God is judging Mammon. What actually is Mammon? Mammon is a world system that is counterfeit to the true plan of God for man. Peter Wagner reveals that it is directed by four evil spirits.

1. *The spirit of greed*; this is an excessive desire for material possessions. This creates a sense of well being based upon how many possessions one has.
2. *The spirit of covetousness*; this is a desire for things that are forbidden. This spirit will lead a person into idolatry, or living for things rather than living for God. When you move into idolatry you cannot prosper! The credit card is a major form of idolatry; buying things we cannot afford.
3. *The spirit of parsimony;* this is being stingy or being a miser. This manifests in hoarding, being a pack rat. The culture of clutter.
4. *The spirit of self reliance;* "God helps those who help

themselves." This is a false doctrine that tells us we do not need God. This will open the door for people to be angry with God for not providing for them. The truth of the matter is they do not allow God to provide because they are not operating in true faith; they are doing everything by themselves.

Mammon is connected to greed. Greed is connected to fear and fear is ultimately connected to a belief system that there is not going to be enough for us in the end. This is how a person that clearly has more than they will ever need will make poor choices that destroy them. These choices are directed by greed that has convinced them that they will not have enough. Can you think of a famous or rich person who has publically lost everything because of a choice you could see was foolish? We must remember that for every famous person we read about there are regular people like you doing the same thing. Greed can affect a person with millions or pennies.

The avarice lifestyle that connects with greed can never be appeased. No matter how much one has, it will not be enough. Eventually the eyes will see something that the heart decides you cannot live without. The stronghold of greed convinces us to spend money we do not have on these things we do not need. If we cannot get it this way, we will be tempted to illegally obtain it. Why? Because of the power of the spirit of mammon unleashed in the society we live. Not only is this spirit unleashed, it has been the engine of most economic business models of the recent times.

All of this is under God's judgment. He will shake everything that can be shaken so that only the principles that are of Him will remain. If God is shaking and judging Mammon in your life, let go of whatever is connected to the judgment. You will be saved if you let go! Don't look at what you are losing; this is Mammon talking to you. Look at what you are being set free from! This is God speaking to you.

God is freeing us from the things that have captured our passion, time and resources that should be devoted to him. This time of crisis is for everyone to reevaluate their priorities. Jesus said that when we seek the kingdom of God and His righteousness first, all things will be added to our life. This is the priority system we need to put in place.

When we seek the things of this world first and put God last or not at all, this system will be judged as broken and unable to produce life.

What is being removed from you at this time? Can you see the mercy of God being released to you in the midst of your crisis? Begin to thank God that He is allowing you to be free of those things that will eventually destroy you. God wants you to turn from the power of Mammon and trust in Him. He is asking you to repent, or make a one hundred and eighty degree turn. Quit following this world and start submitting to Him. When this happens, you will see all aspects of your life start to turn for the better.

Overcoming the Spirit of Poverty

God wants us to prosper in all aspects of life. This means that we will prosper spiritually because our sins have been forgiven by Jesus Christ. We will prosper physically because He suffered on the cross to take away our infirmities. We will prosper in our minds because He was pierced with a crown of thorns around His mind. Our emotions should prosper because His emotions were crushed for our iniquities. We should prosper financially because He became poor that we could become rich! When we talk about prosperity or success we are speaking about concepts that are within God's boundaries for our life. It is His will for us to prosper!

Since it is God's will for us to prosper how come so many Christians have difficulty believing this? Dr. C. Peter Wagner says that is because we have a mindset that is controlled by the spirit of poverty...

> *To move into wealth, we must break out of the mindset and spirit of poverty. We must move beyond the old religious mindsets that will hinder our faith and stop us from moving into our destiny. God has new ways to get finances to us. Let's break the spirit of poverty!*

C. Peter Wagner November 12, 2008

When studying the bible it is clear that God has always prospered His people from Abraham in the beginning through Jesus and the early apostles in the New Testament. Many miss the biblical accounts like

44

these and other evidences of how God transferred wealth.

Abraham gained the wealth of the pagan kings. Joseph collected the wealth of all of Egypt. The Jewish slaves left with the gold and jewels of Egypt. David gathered wealth from all the surrounding nations to build the first temple. Nehemiah was given funds from unbelieving nations to build the second temple. Herod built the Temple of Jesus' day. Joseph and Mary were given gifts of great wealth when the Wise Men came to worship Jesus. This wealth must have been very substantial.

Jesus had a group of women including the wife of Herod's treasurer that helped to support His itinerant ministry. The early church had wealth that was able to be distributed to care for the poor, the widows, and even survive a famine. There is a clear picture of sufficient wealth for great offerings to be sent by Paul from one city to another. Land was sold and laid at the apostles feet for wise distribution.

The picture we see from scripture is the church had the resources to do the things we now expect the government to do for us. When I read all of these stories I am filled with faith to believe we will have enough money to spread the gospel to the nations in our day. God was able to communicate with His people to use the wealth for His glory and to expand His kingdom. The spirit of poverty has veiled our eyes from these great examples of provision that have already taken place and it is time for us to ask God to remove this veil.

The spirit of poverty in the church has delayed the transfer of wealth promised to us in the bible. It was in the early 1990's that prophets started telling us that great wealth will be released. Why has God waited so long to do this? Could it be that God's people are not ready for this shift? Some will see the transfer of wealth and some will not. Why; because those who have a spirit of poverty will not be able to get the finances. The spirit of poverty will stop faith from operating in the heart of that believer. You can have faith for your eternal soul to go to heaven but this spirit is stopping you from believing that the same God has the power to bring wealth into your life. This type of thinking needs to change!

The spirit of poverty is not only psychological it is demonic. It is

God's will that His people prosper. The first half of the entire chapter of Deuteronomy twenty eight deals with the spirit of prosperity. The second half deals with the spirit of poverty. Prosperity is a blessing and poverty is a curse. The New Testament is also filled with examples of how God wants us to prosper. It is a demonic power to get us to believe that we are being spiritual when we are poor and suffering. It is demonic to think that a good God would rejoice in His children suffering and starving while billions of dollars are spent on sinful activities every day. This is another example of how Christians can call something evil good. All of this is connected to a scheme or device to stop us from advancing the kingdom of God. It is time to agree that poverty is of the devil and prosperity is of God!

How did the spirit of poverty become so powerfully entrenched in the minds of believers today? It started with medieval monasticism. The curse of medieval monasticism came in during this time through the monastery mindset as opposed to the prosperity mindset. The clergy had to take three vows: Poverty, Chastity and Obedience. This separation between clergy and laity has brought a curse that we are still breaking today. These vows created the mindset that the priests were to be spiritual not the "regular" people.

The vow of poverty created the mindset that piety is directly proportionate to poverty. The poorer you were, the more spiritual you appeared. Let me ask you right now while you are reading this, do you feel more spiritual when you cannot pay your bills or do the things to expand the kingdom of God that are in your heart? No? Neither do I or most other people. It is a religious spirit working with the poverty spirit to make us believe things we know in practice are not true.

Constantine shifted the church from a Hebrew mindset of prosperity to the Greek mindset: The Hebrew mindset is that everything is connected into a whole. Spiritual things and physical things all belong to God and are to be holy to Him. This protects the heart from idolatry. The Hebrew mind sees the connection between the spiritual and material. The earth is the Lord's and the fullness there of! The Greek mindset believed that the only things that had value were spiritual not material or of the earth. The vow of chastity said that the clergy could not be married or have a family. This was not practiced by the Hebrew priests. The vow of poverty said that the clergy could not have material wealth or possession. The Hebrew Priesthood was in charge of all the wealth of the nation! Even the vow of obedience created a false belief that only the clergy could walk in true obedience to the commands of Christ. God told all the people to obey Him and they would prosper when they entered the Promise Land. The demonic spirit entered the church by separating us from our Jewish roots.

Many Christians have some form of guilt about having wealth. The written and verbal positions of the church since the time of the Reformation have created a mindset that having wealth meant that you did not love God or were not committed to holiness. You could not be spiritual and have money! There are many scriptures warning us about the error of seeking riches over God; but the bible never supports the idea that having wealth is sinful. This came through the traditions handed down to us over the years. The mindset that it is spiritual for preachers to be poor came from this era. This is a mindset that must be broken and overcome for preachers to become leaders of successful people in this day and age.

The church has been breaking free from the spirit of poverty in the last forty years. Each of these steps have brought breakthrough for those who embraced these teachings along with persecution from religious people. *The Word of Faith Movement* led by Kenneth Hagin and others taught the body of Christ about the promises of God regarding wealth and how to bind the spirit of poverty. When they bound this spirit, the people of this movement became prosperous: financially, physically and socially! They have laid an important foundation for us to build upon to be free of poverty.

The second step away from the spirit of poverty and towards the transformation of wealth for our time came with the Social Transformation Movement. The emphasis in theology was to "Take Cities for God" which was promoted by John Dawson in the 1990's. His book spread a theology and created a mindset of taking social units or cities rather than simply reaching individuals. The belief that entire cities could experience the transforming power of the *gospel of the kingdom* became a reality. Transforming entire people groups with all the benefits of the kingdom of God is an essential belief to pull down and destroy the spirit of poverty controlling geographic regions.

Eradicating systemic poverty is the last step in true social transformation. Systemic poverty means that the entire social system people are in is founded in poverty as their way of life. We have to change the social system to systemic prosperity! Prosperity is the social system that creates a mindset expecting to be prosperous instead of expecting to be poor. Singapore is now an example of a nation with systemic prosperity.

Think about systemic poverty in your life. Did you grow up with a mind set that you will always suffer lack? Did you eat rapidly because the food was gone by the time the slow eaters went for seconds? Do you believe you will always have a broken down car? Is your faith level for God to fix the car or replace the car? Do you have faith for God to graduate your kids from college and see them in a successful career? It is important to evict the spirit of poverty from the hearts of believers so we can see it removed from entire communities. This is a very important time to war against this spirit as you navigate the crisis.

The third step in theological understanding to break the spirit of poverty is the *church in the workplace movement.* This movement has been most widely embraced since the beginning of the twenty first century. This movement breaks down the barrier of clergy and laity. It emphasizes that everyone is called to be a minister but the largest percentage of people in the church are called to the market place, not the nuclear church.

How about you? Have you made this shift in your life? Do you think that being spiritual is connected to working at the church alone? Do you see yourself as a minister of the gospel of the kingdom wherever God has planted you? Embracing this theology is essential to navigate the crisis the world is going through. God is planting His kingdom minded people in all spheres of society. Your prosperity will be connected to your willingness to expand the kingdom through your work life. Make a decision that you are going to be spiritual all the time, not just when you go to the church building. You bring the kingdom of God to every place you occupy. You have the ability to change atmospheres and attitudes by the life of God's Spirit inside of you! When you embrace this new identity you will see wealth transferring towards you. Declare that you will be a steward of wealth in this new season! It is godly to be a steward of wealth through the different markets in the world.

The church is currently entering the season of the *Transfer of Wealth*. The prophets have been saying that it is God's desire that huge amounts of wealth should be transferred into the kingdom of God. If this is true, why has this not taken place? By studying the past three moves of God over the last forty years, we can see that the church is closer to seeing a modern move of this biblical principle as a reality than ever before. Here are some keys to see the transfer of wealth become a reality.

We need to change our minds so God can release this to us. We will not see wealth come into our lives if we do not express true faith for it to happen. You must move beyond wishful thinking into a place of assured expectation. We must change our minds about wealth itself. We cannot be in judgment against people with wealth in our thoughts and speech and then think that wealth will enter into our lives. We must respect the power of wealth and what it can accomplish. There are many thoughts controlled by the spirit of poverty and Mammon that we need to repent of in order for us to see wealth come our way. Make a decision and then start saying out loud, "I am changing my mind regarding wealth!"

The biblical government of the church must be properly established. In 2001 the second apostolic age began. This represents the first time since the early church government that all five ascension gifts are recognized and working together in the church. The advancement of the kingdom of God is connected to building the church according to God's biblical design. It is necessary for the church to be correctly fit together for every joint to receive the supply from every part of the body. When we are missing parts of the body of Christ our supply is hindered. When we are correctly fit together, our supply flows freely in. Make a declaration that you will embrace all the ministries and gifts of God through His people in your life today. This opens the gates of supply for the transfer of wealth.

The bible states that the church is founded upon apostles and prophets. Don't allow the use of biblical words to throw you off. Think of it in this way. Do you know anyone that has an innate ability for business timing? Do you know anyone that knows how to put business plans into effect and reality? These are examples to be prophetic or apostolic. I am not saying that everyone like this is an apostle or prophet, but those who are have these abilities. There is a heavenly revelation, timing and ability to join people and resources which are essential in the transfer of wealth. This is an important step in experiencing our destiny. This statement is true for everyone regardless if they are in the church world or in the workplace.

If you are going to participate in the transfer of wealth you need to be correctly aligned. We have already discussed that this is the year to align. This will help you hear what to do, when to do it, and how to put it together right. Alignment with people that can hear what to do and those who know how to make it work are essential. Make sure you are connected to people who are positive and believing; even if right now they are not believers in Jesus! God wants us to work together in the world to make a difference in the life of everyone. Attitude will determine altitude in this time. Get properly connected on all fronts so you can start to experience the provision God has for you to steward.

Being in the right place at the right time is crucial in this hour. The old adage of real estate; location, location, location applies to your ability to see the transfer of wealth. God has a field for you to sow in. He has a harvest for you to reap. The crisis is realigning people into different geographic regions and different jobs. Don't resist the flow of God's opportunity. Stay positive and look for the right field to move into at this time. New fields will be opening and old fields are closing. Your field is connected to your alignment.

Informed intercession through workplace intercessors is going to be necessary for the transfer of wealth in your realm of business. We used to think we did all our praying at the church on Sunday. Now it is time to change your attitude about prayer at your workplace. Think about what stops big projects from succeeding. It is usually not the idea or concept; it is a few details along the way. It could be a signature that is missing because one person won't sign. It could be one part of the process that engineering cannot get to function. God wants these specific events to be covered in prayer by people that know how to pray.

Intercession is a spiritual gift. Everyone is called to pray but some people pray more effectively than others. To see the transfer of wealth come into your business you need to have a place in your business that the right people who are kingdom minded can come into agreement for progress and success. You need to have intercessors that believe for you to prosper over specific moments in the life of the business. Some businesses have such an understanding about this concept that they are employing people with the spiritual gift to pray for the business just as if they were employing an administrative associate in the company!

As an apostle or leader in the church world, I stand in intercessory agreement with the business people who are aligned and submitted in my realm of authority. One of the workplace leaders wrote to me about a new opportunity that had opened up for him in an email. I had prophesied over his family publically the week prior. This was a confirmation of what I had spoken. Rather than making a remark of that being a good thing, I wrote my intercession prayer and decreed it for his success. Here is what I prayed and wrote…

> Dear Carl:
> I am so thankful for this first fruits of opportunity for 2009. I am committed to pray for you and be there for you in the spirit realm as you break forth and shine with HIS glory. You are truly a blessing in my life.
>
> Father we agree together that you have opened this door of opportunity. I declare that every demonic hindrance in Palmdale be dethroned by the Blood of Jesus Christ and the victory of the cross. I ask that the angelic hosts be sent to clear the atmosphere when Carl speaks. I declare that the words in Carl's mouth will be the voice of God and bring hope to all the people. I declare that success factors will come into Carl's path during this trip. In the Name of Jesus.

This type of interaction must become a regular part of how we interact in the future. It is important to have specific informed intercession from both the spiritual alignment and on the ground in your business environments. This type of prayer alliance will move the enemies that are planted in the gates of kingdom financial prosperity in your business arena.

There is a "strong man" that needs to be bound who is standing in your gate of kingdom supply. Jesus said that we have to bind up the strong man before we can take the spoils of his house. In practical terms this means that our prayers need to focus on the strong points of resistance that are hindering our success. Generalized prayers will not break this stronghold. Ask for heavenly insight and specific words to pray. These are the keys to victory. When I pray for a man to be free from addiction to alcohol I usually pray for the painful wounds in his life to be healed. The alcohol is his medicine for the pain. When he understands the source of the pain and gets help, he is then able to be free of the alcohol. This is how informed, prophetic, apostolic intercession works. You are aligning the spiritual gifts God has designed inside of people with spiritual insights to the root sources that are holding things back. This type of prayer is the heavenly arsenal that God has designed to pull down the strong resistance that often can cause financial failure.

The final aspect in seeing the transfer of wealth become a reality in your life is based in your covenant with God Himself. God has a stake in you being successful. You are a reflection of His ability to do things with your life that causes others to see Him in a different light. When David fought the giant he approached the enemy with confidence. He said out loud that the source of his victory was based in his covenant alignment with Almighty God. He knew his God was going to keep up His end of the covenant. David's responsibility was to go forward and fight. When you go forward in your business with faith in God you are giving Him something to work with! God will use your victory as a window for others to see how He works in the life of a regular person. Have faith in your covenant with God to see the transfer of wealth take place in your life.

In the end, the transfer of wealth will come in three ways. The first will be supernatural transfer. This means that God will give you money you did not earn. Doorways of supply will come into your life in ways you never thought possible. Don't close doors that are trying to open for you in this season. They may have a great amount of wealth coming in behind them!

Self reliance will keep this door shut. How many times has someone tried to bless you and you say, "No thanks, I will take care of that myself." Every time we refuse to accept help we are closing the door. God has created us to work with each other, not all alone. You may have been hurt, burned, etc in the past but refuse to become a loner. The times that we are entering must be navigated by working together. Joining gifts and talents to find success is the way to see wealth transferred into your life.

 False humility can keep the gates of supply closed in your future. False humility is expressed in different ways that seem like you are being a good person. You may be the one who always picks up the check but will never let someone else treat you. You may have someone wanting to bless you with a gift and you refuse to accept it. God created us to receive. We must receive from God and we need to receive from our fellow man. When we learn to truly humble ourselves we can accept a gift. We simply need to graciously say, "Thank you." This is how humility will allow you to participate in the transfer of wealth.

Another way that the transfer of wealth will come into your life is by God giving you the ability to create wealth. I am going to spend an entire chapter explaining this concept later in the book. This is easiest explained by the Lord showing you how to be successful in business. Being your own boss will be the best way for wealth to shift into your life.

The final or third way that wealth will transfer from unrighteous hands into those of the righteous will be a combination of both of the above. God can bring finances to you that you did not work for and He can bring in wealth that is a complete surprise to you. Be ready for it to take place in one fashion or another. Start to ask God to help you be a part of this incredible event. He will begin to show you how.

God transferred wealth to Israel in this combination method when they left Egypt under Moses. The people were slaves with a generational heritage of slavery. For over four hundred years this was the only lifestyle Israel understood. You might identify with this type of heritage in your life. When God had the Israelites leave, they were given all manner of gold, silver, and precious elements out of the earth from those who owned them.

Later when they crossed the Jordon River, they would be given houses, lands, vineyards and fields that they did not build or plant. They received something by grace but it required that same grace to learn how to farm that land once they crossed the river. This is a great picture from the scriptures of how God will transfer wealth once again in our time. It might start supernaturally for many because we do not have a heritage of wealth from our family. Later God will make us responsible to start creating wealth. In both cases the wealth transfer is because of the mercy of God. Are you ready to be a steward of this mercy?

Remember, the reason that wealth is transferring is to see God's kingdom advance. This wealth will go to those who are ready to steward wealth according to His biblical economic principles. You must be willing to be generous with the wealth you have access to now if you expect to see the transfer of wealth come into your life. When the kingdom of God advances everyone prospers. You will be a conduit of wealth; a conveyor belt of supply. If everything coming into your possession goes towards your own personal life, you have missed the true concept of what this is really all about.

Chapter 6

Embracing God's
Purpose and Mission

A Promise and A Warning About Our Future

God was taking Israel out of Egyptian slavery and going to make them a sovereign nation. This period of time is an example of one of the ancient world wide crisis situations that brought a great transfer of wealth. This is documented by the bible and supported by secular history.

The book of Deuteronomy is like a *how to* guide that God had Moses write down for the Israelites to follow and find success in their new society they would create. We must remember that when Deuteronomy was first read by Moses to the people, it spoke about events that were *yet to happen*. It was a prophetic blue print regarding the season that they were about to embark upon. They were in a current place of crisis but the written plan came forth for them to leave the crisis and move into prosperity. They were to be a society of people that reflected the care and provision of Almighty God to all the other nations of the world.

When we read the bible today we are looking back historically and we see that everything God told them would happen actually did take place. God gave them more than a plan to get out of their crisis, He also wrote down the pitfalls that would come with their success. He warned them regarding how their hearts would get proud and they would leave God's ways as their only standard of practice. I am very aware of this dynamic of God as I write this book. I am using the scriptural principles for us to learn what to do to get out of our crisis and what to do to stay out of a future crisis. This is worth reading and pondering for any person regardless if they are currently a believer in Jesus Christ or not.

As the book of Deuteronomy goes along God gives the people a very stern warning. He warns them that things will become so successful they could forget how this all started. They could start to think they became a success apart from God. They could start doing things with their wealth that no longer honors God.

As I read this historic book of the bible it makes me think about America. America was founded by a dream God had for a nation. The early success of this nation was not founded in the riches of kings it was founded by the promise of God placed into the hearts of courageous men and women. They risked their lives to find a place that was free to worship the Lord Jesus Christ and His Father the creator of heaven and earth. They did not have a dream birthed out of materialism, atheism or pluralism. They were delivered from one place of persecution through the wilderness of early hardships and by 1776 they forged a nation dependent upon Almighty God. All of this is recorded in their own historical documents.

As our history continued we can look back at the great wars America has fought, i.e. the crisis of the Great Depression, and see all have a common thread of extended success as a nation leading into self indulgence which would end in a national crisis. We as an American people and even most of the Western world is currently guilty of experiencing financial success while excluding God from our conversation, conduct or charters. This rapid movement to remove God from our midst has been accompanied with a rapid downfall of society and finally economic destruction.

All nations have a God given dream in their creation just like America. In their history and charters are stories of destiny, courage and sacrifice. When they were founded they were founded upon God's dream. When they failed they left the pathway of His dream. When we leave our destiny to pursue another dream we will always fail.

We cannot lose sight of the fact that God's dream for America is the seed for the future success of our country. God has used the crisis in times past to bring people back to a proper understanding of righteousness, holiness and purpose. It brought about a reconnecting or reforming of society to be God centered rather than man centered.

I write all this historic information to say this; there is a great tension between the success that God created man to know and how man forgets God when he prospers. This thought leads to the reason that we are going to study this portion of scripture in this chapter. There are many parallels for us to examine and principles regarding God's covenant that we need to establish in our hearts during this season in order for us to move forward into our next season. God wants us to prosper but it is for the purpose of promoting His ultimate dream for the nations of the world. When we fail to live His dream we will fail in the crisis we create.

Deuteronomy 8:7-18 (NASB)

[7] *"For the Lord your God is bringing you into a good land, a land of brooks of water, of fountains and springs, flowing forth in valleys and hills;*
[8] *a land of wheat and barley, of vines and fig trees and pomegranates, a land of olive oil and honey;*
[9] *a land where you will eat food without scarcity, in which you will not lack anything; a land whose stones are iron, and out of whose hills you can dig copper.*

Verses seven through nine give us a prophetic picture of God's plan to bring blessing to a group of people who were once slaves and suffering. They were currently wandering aimlessly and suffering in the desert when the book of Deuteronomy was first written for them to read. This was their word they had to have while in their wilderness season. This was the transition time where they wanted to go back to the slavery of Egypt. In many ways our old life always looks better when we forget the true suffering we had back then. They could not go back and they did not want to stay where they were. They needed a clear word of direction on what to do and where to go. God brought them this incredibly encouraging word to motivate them to go forward and overcome their current fears.

Look at the promise of verse seven; God is bringing you into a good land. This is God's heart and motivation for all of us. He is a good God who wants to see us succeed. He is taking responsibility for our arrival at our new destination. He is clarifying that the new land is a good land. It might seem scary to step out and do things you have not done before, but He is asking us to grasp His hand and start moving forward towards something good. This is what the word of the Lord will look like when we are spoken to in our hour.

Verses seven, eight and nine all have something very important in common. The good that God is bringing them into comes out of the land itself. The new ideas and solutions for us today are connected to the earth and what is coming out of the earth. People will be saying that *green jobs* are the wave of the future. Even the unbeliever has insight in this hour. This is how God brings wealth and restoration; it comes out of the earth!

The promise of God to the people of covenant was that they would eat without scarcity. This is the complete opposite of the spirit of fear that we are facing as a society right now. Everyone fears scarcity. There is not enough to go around so we better hoard what we have access to. No! Move in the opposite direction and create a mentality of abundance. This is your word to move into your future.

Generosity is the nature of our Father. We are not to be wasteful of God's resources. The current judgment of mammon is connected to waste. Allow God to go through your check book and tell you where your money needs to stop going. In this new season we are to be generous. Give lavishly to kingdom causes because you will be eating abundantly. How would you give if you knew that your bank account would not go empty? What will you give to in this new season? Remember this word was a prophetic word when Israel first heard it! Declare out loud that you are going to generously give to all the kingdom causes God reveals to your heart!

Verse nine tells us that *we will dig*. This is another important aspect of moving out of today's crisis. We live in an age where we do not want to be responsible for our own lives or actions. People want someone else to dig for them. Laws are written and interpreted in today's courts making irresponsible people beneficiaries of the labor of other people. This may have worked for a while, but this is not God's way of prosperity. If a person does not work they should not eat. Work is God's will and He wants us to partake of it. You will never leave your wilderness by remaining irresponsible. Declare that you will dig and you will find new resources of wealth that God is now opening up to you! Tell your body and mind that you are going to go to work and prosper. Your future wealth is connected to your willingness to dig where God sends you.

> *[10] "When you have eaten and are satisfied, you shall bless the Lord your God for the good land which He has given you.*

Verse ten gives us another key principle of how to move into our new season. We are commanded to bless the Lord when we have eaten and are satisfied. Blessing and honoring God is not an option. We are to bless Him with our lips, our lives, our worship and our wealth. I have seen people who have moved from seasons of crisis to prosperity and get so busy prospering they do not worship God. I see people living in the crisis right now that are not honoring God with their lips. They are murmuring and complaining about everyone around them. This attitude will never allow you to eat and be satisfied! Stop griping and start praising God for a good word that you are going to be satisfied. Make a decision right now to start praising God and speaking blessing about everyone with which He has aligned you. Declare that you are going into a good land that God has given you. You will eat and be satisfied.

> *[11] "Beware that you do not forget the Lord your God by not keeping His commandments and His ordinances and His statutes which I am commanding you today;*

> *[12] otherwise, when you have eaten and are satisfied, and have built good houses and lived in them,*

Here comes a very important warning for us as we leave our crisis and wilderness. God connects the obedience of today with our ability to staying connected and faithful to Him for the long term. People think they can take time off from obeying God. They think it is okay because they seem to get away with it when they do. This is deceptive. Every time we excuse ourselves from obeying God's principles our hearts become less sensitive to the Holy Spirit. You can be so desensitized to the grieving of the Holy Spirit that you will think everything is great between you and God while walking in open disobedience to His written principles.

Watch out! This is why God warned the people in advance. Things could start getting better and we stop realizing why things actually improved. There is a connection between doing what God wants us to do on a daily basis and the quality of our lives that we experience. There is a time factor involved in all of this as well. Usually, as a rule of thumb, today's disobedience does not bring sorrow or trouble to us immediately. This is why we can fail to realize how many of God's principles we are disregarding. It becomes a habit to have partial obedience which will lead to disobedience.

Finally after a few weeks or months, the fruit of these bad decisions will catch up to us. Life can go bad quickly once it starts going bad. The self deception that my disobedience had no consequences has a price to pay. Getting out of the wilderness of crisis is connected to hearing God's word or plan and obeying it. Step by step, day by day, obedience will result in a new season of God's great provision. If you stop listening and obeying, step by step, day by day you will go back into a different and new crisis. God warns us before we succeed that there is only one way to stay successful. Listen and obey every day.

The warning in verse twelve shows how deception can enter our lives. We are obedient at the beginning and the prophetic promises will be experienced. People can look at the benefits of their life and say, "I am obeying God. Look at everything I have to prove it." There is a blind spot in the hearts of people to see that today's fruit is the result of yesterday's obedience. What we are sowing right now may not have fruit showing at this time, but it will spring forth.

Ask God to reveal to you every day before you go to bed what written principles you have violated. Your mind will want to justify why you disobeyed. It was someone's fault that you judged them or something like that. Refuse to justify disobedience with your circumstances. Take responsibility and ask forgiveness from God. The next step is to humble yourself and ask forgiveness of the person you sinned against. Even if you think it is their fault, take responsibility for your actions, words or deeds. If it was simply your thoughts, don't trouble them. Repent of the thoughts and take them captive by refusing to *nurse and rehearse* your offenses.

> *[13] and when your herds and your flocks multiply, and your silver and gold multiply, and all that you have multiplies,*
> *[14] then your heart will become proud and you will forget the Lord your God who brought you out from the land of Egypt,*

out of the house of slavery.

The warning continues in verses thirteen and fourteen along with an incredible promise. God is willing to multiply our flocks, silver, gold and everything we have. What an incredible thought. God would be willing to do this even when He knows that some will get filled with pride and forget Him. We start telling everyone about ourselves instead of remembering that it all started with God. I was once a slave without hope of anything changing. God started me on a journey because of His grace and mercy. Anything I did along the way was because He gave me the grace to do it.

Over time we can become so prosperous that pride enters into our lives. If this happens, we can fall into the trap of replacing God with our soulish ambitions that begin to change our focus and desires. We must guard against this by realizing that God blesses us for a greater purpose than this. We are blessed to be stewards of wealth to advance His kindgom and values. We are to be an example of God's grace to change a life from poverty and slavery into multipled abundance. God warns us that our future prosperity could open the door to forgetting where our true wealth originated. Declare in your daily prayers that God is the reason for your blessings and give Him honor every day.

> [15] *"He led you through the great and terrible wilderness, with its fiery serpents and scorpions and thirsty ground where there was no water; He brought water for you out of the rock of flint.*
> [16] *"In the wilderness He fed you manna which your fathers did not know, that He might humble you and that He might test you, to do good for you in the end.*
> [17] *"Otherwise, you may say in your heart, 'My power and the strength of my hand made me this wealth.'*

Verses fifteen and sixteen remind us of what it is like for us in the wilderness from God's perspective. Have you ever stopped to think that there is another view of what you are going through rather than your own? Remember, the big picture principle. Historically God uses wilderness experiences to move us from one season into the next. The wilderness is the time in between and it has a very important purpose to move us to a new level of faith to succeed in the new season. God says that the wilderness time is great and terrible. He is very aware of how painful this time in your life is.

I know some that fall away from the faith during wilderness seasons because they think God has stopped caring. They feel that God has left them to perish. He knows that the elements of your circumstances sting with pain. The poison of your experiences has left you feeling week and sick. This is a crucial time to take note. Some might fall away from the faith during this part of the wilderness and others enter into judgments against their fellow man. It is as if we cannot be mad at God so we take it out on the people around us.

The fiery serpents that are spoken about in this scripture came upon the people because they murmured and complained against God and His leader Moses openly. If you want to learn something about getting out of the wilderness you are currently in learn this; murmuring is going to get you into more trouble with God than any other thing. Murmuring is an interesting word in the Hebrew language. It is a picture of the lonesome dove in the desert crying a song for its mate. It wants to make others feel sorry for you because your life is so bad. "Woe is me, no one cares about me." This is what brought snakes into the camp and people started to die from the poison!

God gave them a solution to save their life in that time of crisis. He made a bronze serpent and had it put on a pole. Everyone who would look at that serpent would be healed and those who refused died. Can you imagine the inner turmoil? You are sick and dying from the bite of a snake and now God wants you to look at a snake? The snake was the symbol of the penalty for their murmuring. They had to acknowledge their actions and words; their part of the problem had to be accepted. In the wilderness we can say that other people are the snakes in our lives. We can blame our problems on them but in reality the wilderness is a place of testing. Will you obey the principles of God's word even when your circumstances bring you pain? Look at your pain through the choices you have made and forget about everyone around you. This is how the fatal poison in your heart will be healed by the mercy of God. Forgive those who have hurt you and move forward into a season of multiplied blessings.

The words of our mouth will either justify us or condemn us before God. The last warning God gives to us here is that we would *say in our heart*. This means that we may not even say it to someone else. We believe inside of our own hearts that God did not get me out of the crisis, I had to do it all by myself. Some people will never leave the wilderness because they cannot get beyond their own emotions and feelings. The wilderness is where we learn it really is not all about me. It is about my God and His plan for the world that He allows me to be a part of. If this part is as big as I want or as small as He wants, I will be thankful and glad to be a part of His plan instead of suffering in the wilderness. I am going to be quiet and submit to God and my leaders with a good attitude because I don't want to stay in the wilderness nor do I want to go back there any time soon!

Everything in this chapter of Deuteronomy up to this point is a combination of a warning and a promise. The promise is that God is going to move us forward and the warning is that we need to honor and obey Him when it happens. The next verse is a very important word that we need to get into our hearts if we are going to participate in the transfer of wealth. It is a word that will break the poverty spirit off your life. It is a word that will give you a strategy to be righteous and prosper in your new season. It is a word that can be the key to move you into your new season of God's supply.

The Power to Get Wealth

God is judging the spirit of Mammon. This is the best time for this teaching about wealth to come forward. If you do not break free of the spirit of mammon in this season you might lose everything because mammon is going to fail. In this season of God judging mammon I need to get as far away from the spirit of mammon, the system of mammon, as possible. This is the season to give more away than any other time in our life. In a time of difficulty there can be breakthrough and restoration or the reconstitution of God through giving.

Dutch Sheets November 13, 2008

Deuteronomy 8:18 (KJV)
18 But thou shalt remember the LORD thy God: for *it is* he that ***giveth*** thee ***power*** to ***get*** wealth, that he may establish his ***covenant*** which he sware unto thy fathers, as *it is* this day.

This verse is a very important word that allows us to participate in the transfer of wealth. It is a word that will break the poverty spirit off the church and it will give us a strategy for our new season. It is a word that will open the gates of God's supply. Ask God to open your mind to His Spirit right now before you read any further. Declare that you are going to see this verse with God's purpose for your life!

In this verse of scripture we see that it is God's plan to prosper us in our society. God was telling Israel that He was making a covenant with them so that they would prosper as a nation among all the other nations. There was a time for four hundred years that there was no nation called Israel. Now God was going to give them a strategy to create a prosperous society. He was taking them out of their slavery and He would cause all the surrounding nations to stop and marvel. The God of Israel is the great One of all the nations of the earth.

This is what God is doing with us today. The transfer of wealth is not about you or me getting rich or retiring early. There is an eternal redemptive purpose for the nations of the earth connected to this plan. It requires wealth to expand God's kingdom. Jesus told a parable about how kings count their money before they go to war. For the last four hundred years the reformed church has lived under the spirit of poverty and lacked the resources to fulfill the mandate to make disciples of all the nations of the earth. Now is the time for the slavery to poverty to end and the gates of supply to open. Declare that you are going to be a part of this triumphant people in the last days!

There are four key words for us to examine in this passage of scripture: give, power, get and covenant. The first word to look at is *give*. This word in the Hebrew literally means that it is an assignment. Most people think that wealth creation is something *other people* do. If you are in covenant with God through your faith in Jesus Christ guess what; you are one of those other people. When we think of it as an assignment we start to look at wealth differently than simply finding a way to pay our bills. We have a reason to be financially successful while living on the earth as a child of God.

I know many well meaning and committed people who love God but never approached wealth as an assignment from God. In fact, the religious spirit may have some thinking they are more spiritual than others because they can be content in an atmosphere of lack. In reality the curse is represented by lack; creating wealth is our covenant assignment while on the earth. If The Lord your God gives you this assignment, what do you want to do before you meet Him in heaven one day? Stop right now and declare, I will accept my assignment from God to create wealth for the kingdom of God.

We must prosper so His covenant will go into all the earth. The assignment to gain wealth is not a lucky break for a few people. It is literally God's plan for you when you enter into His family. The scriptures teach us that God gives us the responsibility to prosper because it is the only way that He can get His covenant into all the earth. The gospel of the kingdom will be preached to all the nations before Jesus returns. It will take kingdom wealth to overcome the kingdom of darkness in our day.

The second key word in this passage is *power*. We usually think of power like the word used to describe dynamite or energy. We think about blowing something up or turning something on. This is not the case in this instance. This word for power means the ability to change and adapt in a changing environment. It literally was used to describe the chameleon lizards in the wilderness with the people in that day. They were aware of these lizards that could change color with their surroundings to blend in and survive. They did more than survive, they multiplied!

The power God is giving us is the ability to adapt to the surrounding economy and prosper. Old economic models that are no longer relevant are not our source of inspiration. We are going to get new innovations from heaven for this new season. No matter what is going on around us God has given us the ability to adapt and change. I am going to prosper in this season because I am distancing myself from the ways of mammon. When God judges mammon we can change in our beliefs and practices that are not righteous. No matter what happens around me, God is going to change me and cause me to prosper. Declare that new ideas from heaven are emerging right now in your life.

The third key word in our passage is the word we translate as *get*. This is a small word with a powerful message. This word literally means to conceive through supernatural creativity. There are going to be new ideas from heaven emerging into your life in this new season; ideas that do not fit into the old wine skins or ways of thinking in the past. These ideas are the creative seeds of heaven being planted in your heart for the new season you are about to emerge victoriously into.

You need to become pregnant with God's assignment! God is going to birth something new inside of you. The God type of DNA that is so alive and so full of power is coming to you in this new season. He will break forth and give birth to something greater than a mere human could conceive. We are called to be supernatural people. God declares, "I am going to give you the ability to keep on creating wealth regardless of what is going on around you."

Remember birth is connected to passion. You are going to be passionate about ideas that will give birth and bring forth fruit in the years to come. What is creating a passion in your heart that is tied to creating wealth? Refuse to be tied to old ways that are no longer bearing financial fruit in your life. It is the mercy of God for some of you that your old season has closed beyond your ability to keep it going. Let go of the past. Mourn for a moment, and now move on! Stop right now and declare that your mind will receive the new creativity that is coming to you from heaven. Thank God for the new ideas that will produce wealth in your assignment.

The fourth and last key word in our scripture is *covenant*. Four hundred years before Deuteronomy was written God made a covenant with Abraham to bless all the nations of the earth. Jesus is the ultimate fulfillment of that promise. When you entered into Jesus Christ through faith, you became a steward of that covenant. Covenant means a lot to God. It means that we are now His responsibility to see that every promise made to us and through us will be fulfilled. He takes this very seriously and so should we. When we prosper in the right way with the right attitude we are a reflection of God's covenant power to keep us and take care of us. When we accomplish great feats to expand the kingdom of God the world is going to marvel at our God.

One day I was worshipping and the Spirit of the Lord asked me, "What is it that I could do through you that would make your entire city stop and marvel at My great ability?" This question caused me to stop singing and start listening. God never asks a question because He does not know the answer. He asks a question because I don't know the answer and He wants to tell me! The words He spoke to my heart caused me to tremble. Even now I don't have the liberty to write it out for others to read and judge. The Holy Spirit wants me to wait until others start flowing in their assignments to create wealth. When they do and they ask me what we are going to do to bless our city, I know what the answer will be! It requires great wealth to bless others with the kingdom of God. This is why we are required to create wealth! Here is our passage again with my notes included next to the words we studied.

Deuteronomy 8:18 (KJV)

18 But thou shalt remember the LORD thy God: for it is he that *giveth (my assignment on earth before I go to heaven)* thee *power (the ability to adapt and change regardless of circumstances)* to *get (give birth through supernatural creativity)* wealth, that he may establish his *covenant* (the blessings of all the nations with the knowledge and power of the kingdom of God) which he sware unto thy fathers, as it is this day.

Now that you have a new view of God's plan for your life and gaining wealth you need a new prayer strategy. Start every day by making this confession over your life until you move into your new season with God's provision.

My confession to succeed

- *I will find, know and accept my assignment from the Father*
- *I will accept God's ability to change regardless of my circumstances and move forward into His plan for my life.*
- *I will give birth through supernatural ability to the vision He is giving me.*

- *I will succeed because I am in covenant with the Father through Jesus Christ.*

Chapter 7

Alignment in the Crisis

The Modern Day Apostolos

The Apostolos is to take the culture of heaven into the sphere on earth that God has assigned you. Regardless of where you are at in the sphere, if you are of the Apostolos you have the anointing to change the culture.

Lance Wallnau November 13, 2008

The church is going into a season of radical change. This change is going to affect the way she sees herself, her mission and her effectiveness reaching the world. This is not a change from the original mission to go and make disciples of the entire world that Jesus gave to us when He ascended into heaven. The change is in how the church is approaching this mission.

The last great revival in America that was marked by a significant number of people being born again and believing in the power of the Holy Spirit goes back to the 1960's and 1970's. It was during this time the theology and purpose of those new believers were influenced by the teaching that the rapture of the church could take place at any moment.

I believe in the biblical teaching of the rapture of the church. I believe in the literal return of Jesus Christ. Unfortunately, the long term effects of waiting on the rapture has affected the churches ability to influence and shape society. It seemed that the worse things would be the church would rejoice because it must mean that we are closer to the return of Christ. How bad can it get and why are we still here?

This is our current wilderness and our current test. We now have a clear word about our mission. The church is here to influence people for good and we are to push back the darkness and evil of the world until Christ returns. He is returning for a victorious overcoming church! We should be working together as one to see darkness pushed back and entire nations changed by the glory of God before the Lord returns.

A new wineskin is emerging to bring the gospel of the kingdom to all the nations of the world through leaders who will go into every sphere of culture to influence their world with the values of the kingdom. This new paradigm gives everyone a calling to go forward and share the gospel not only the clergy. It gives every believer a place and purpose to expand the kingdom outside of the church building on Sunday morning.

This moves most Christians from being observers to participants. Wherever you work you can fulfill your calling just as much as a pastor or person who works at the local church. God is calling us all to grasp this vision as a part of the new change that is taking place. This move is going to change the way the church looks to those on the other side of this current chasm. We are being called and sent to reflect Jesus in our beliefs, character and conduct. This new group is the Lord's *modern apostolos*.

Jesus called His first disciples which traveled with Him *apostles*. This word that He used was a military word; apostolos. It was originally used to describe the armada of ships that would bring all the necessary people to a new land and develop and build the culture of the king in that new land. They were given a blue print by the king and they committed themselves to see it become a reality in the new province. When the Phoenician army had conquered a new territory, they *sent* those who would bring the new education, government, business, and other key changes to that society.

Sent is the literal word for apostle, and this is the context of the assignment Jesus gave His twelve disciples. They went from being trained by observation to being sent to manifest God's kingdom in the surrounding regions. This group was sent out by Jesus to change the spiritual atmosphere and allow the people to experience the culture of their new king. They would learn the benefits of the new king from these sent leaders who travelled together into their land. The apostolos were ambassadors of change. They travelled together into every part of society and brought kingdom power, a kingdom message and kingdom values to manifest God's blessings to all the people.

When Jesus made the prayerful decision to call His twelve disciples apostles, it also reflected a shift in His ministry due to a crisis. Up to that point in time Jesus did the ministry and the disciples watched and learned. The political climate changed and the chief priests and scribes began to conspire how to put Jesus to death. He spent the night in prayer and came forward with a new strategy from heaven.

He called the apostles, or apostolos, and *sent* them two by two into the cities *before* He entered the city. The apostles brought the culture of heaven to the villages on earth. They changed the spiritual atmosphere of the cities with the power of the kingdom of God. This was their assignment. God's answer to that crisis is the same as our current crisis. Multiply the teams of people who are manifesting His kingdom. When the enemy wants to stop the move of God, multiply those who are sent and advance.

We are now in the second apostolic era of the church. Jesus is sending us to every sector of society to show people on earth what heaven looks like. This means that the assignment of God for you will be connected to being a part of His apostolos. God is sending you to let people experience His love, peace and joy through your life wherever you work. He is not asking you to become the office preacher; He is going to use you as a person of His presence in the office. He will do the rest.

One of the people that has been speaking on this new paradigm for the church is Lance Wallnau. Lance tells the story of how he came to study the topic that we now call, *The Seven Mountain Mandate*. It is important to understand the Seven Mountain Mandate because it is connected to God's purpose for the church in this hour. I am going to quickly give an overview of this story that I have heard Lance tell on several occasions. Many modern teachers are referencing it. Knowing this story will help you grasp God's modern mission for you to follow.

There is a man by the name of Michael Crotts. He was running for the office of State Senator in Georgia when he suffered a massive heart attack and died for thirty three minutes while doctors and paramedics tried to revive him. His wife continued to pray for him to live while the doctors seemed to have no success bringing him back to life. During this time frame, Jesus came to Michael and began to speak to him about his future. They were walking together in front of some mountains. There was one huge mountain that was larger than the seven smaller mountains that were at its base. Jesus pointed to this mountain and told him that it was the kingdom of God which is greater than any other kingdom. The seven smaller mountains represented the seven spheres of influence that control the thinking of the people on the earth. The Lord told Michael that whoever controlled the tops of these seven mountains would control the harvest of the nations. He then pointed towards one mountain and told him that he was to go to the mountain called government. This was his mountain. He would pave the way during his life for his son to advance even further up to the top of this mountain.

At the end of this conversation Michael's wife who was still praying over her dead husband's body commanded his spirit to come return into his body. He then left the mountains and the conversation with Jesus and returned into his body alive and well. When he spoke to his wife he asked her, "Where is our son Caleb?" At that time they did not have a son, but the conversation with Jesus was so real that when he came back to life he was forever changed. Michael went on to win the Senate race and they now have a son named Caleb.

When Lance Wallnau heard this story he began to think about what Jesus had said to Michael Crotts regarding the mountains and the harvest of the nations that was at stake. He began to search out to find the answer to what the other six mountains of culture might be. His journey took him into contact with Loren Cunningham, the founder of Youth with a Mission. Loren told Lance about a meeting he had with Bill Bright, the founder of Campus Crusade for Christ. When these two leaders of the largest youth ministries in the world met, they each came to the meeting with seven areas of influencing culture. One called it the seven mountains of culture and the other called it the seven mind molders of culture. He was astonished that they had each received this information by divine inspiration just prior to their coming together. When they shared the lists the seven areas all matched up identically. Lance had found his answer in this conversation. He now lists the Seven Mountains of modern culture as follows…

1. Religion
2. Family

3. Education
4. Government
5. Marketplace
6. Media
7. Arts

Each of these areas represents a key place of influence and even control of the thinking of the people. Jesus had said that those who control these mountain tops will determine the harvest of the nations of the world. This fits into our biblical mandate to make disciples of all the nations.

It is imperative that the modern day church embrace this mission for our day. We can no longer allow the key sectors of influence in our modern world to be led by people with a world view that marginalizes and disregards God and His plan for man. This leadership has created a mindset for everyone they influence to unknowingly think like their leaders. Current statistics show that roughly one third of Americans believe in God but only about five percent actually have a world view that agrees with God's world view.

This shift in world view is creating the crisis we are experiencing in the world. The strategy to get the whole world moving in the right direction is to see people with kingdom values embrace their calling to move into places of influence. We need to develop a long term strategy to develop a generation of children and youth that are empowered to grow up and become leaders in these seven areas of culture.

This strategy needs to start now as we move out of the crisis. Rather than continually telling the young that Jesus can come back any minute they need to be encouraged that Jesus wants them to find their calling and their mountain. We need to challenge them and support them into developing lifetime dreams of being the leaders on all seven mountains of influence. We cannot judge them as being worldly minded when they say they want to go out from local church to make their mark on the world. We need to support them in prayer and by building their biblical world view before they go out. They need to feel accepted so they continually go in and out as they fulfill their assignment.

We need the existing generations in the workplace to begin to develop strategies which make God relevant to society once again. Jesus said that the end of the age will be identified with a great harvest. We must shift our focus on the return of Jesus to be about the harvest of all the nations rather than the crisis in all the nations. Modern leaders need to develop strategies of how we can go into society and solve modern problems with kingdom solutions.

The world of our day will see the modern Josephs, Esthers and Daniels emerge from obscurity and irrelevance. Daniel was not a Babylonian captive; he was embedded in a nation who did not know God, to reveal to them the True and Living God! The entire nation of Babylon was shifted by Daniel's influence with Nebuchadnezzar. All of Egypt was shifted towards God's righteousness when Joseph emerged from his prison and stepped into the position of Prime Minister. In that day, Pharaoh was known to be a god; but he bowed to Joseph's God!

Looking back at history God has been able raise up leaders from a place of crisis to shift entire nations and people groups in a single generation. This must be the vision, assignment and mission for the church. As we embrace this vision we will be able to leave our modern crisis. We need to see all the existing generations alive today working together. We will develop kingdom strategies to see a great harvest of all the nations of the world before our Lord Jesus Christ returns. If you know a young person even an eight year old boy or girl, I want them to know I believe they will be the leaders of world culture when this great harvest of nations occurs. God is raising up a modern day apostolos who will manifest His kingdom on this earth. They will be successful even if it takes their entire lifetime, it is a noble dream and worthy mission.

In this new season our assignment is to go into all the realms of society and release the culture of God's kingdom. The people of God will be reformers of society by bringing a superior peace, joy and presence into every place God sends us. The key to your success is to understand this new assignment and to be willing to participate. When you catch the vision of being a carrier of God's kingdom to all the nations of the world, you will be able to identify your life purpose.

The modern apostolic era is now upon us. The Lord is sending us to shape entire nations one sphere at a time. Together we are the armada of believers that bring the supernatural culture of God's kingdom into the places we work every day. Start gathering other believers and share this vision with them. God's kingdom is inside of all of you who believe. God wants you to release it to allow others to see the real Jesus. It may sound like a huge undertaking but it's already at work all over the world. Make a declaration that you will become a part of the Lord's apostolos today!

The Shift from Shepherd to General

Spiritual warfare has prayer, petition, declaration and decrees. It includes the help of angels as we have seen. It also includes having the courage to take action when it is time to do so. There are times to pray and times to move. Those who only pray and never move will never leave their wilderness. The crisis is something you are moving out of, not something you are going to spend your lifetime praying about. If you are going to move into your new season you must take decisive actions in embracing God's new identity for your life.

One of the great shifts in history was the shift of leadership from Moses to Joshua. Moses was a shepherd leader while Joshua was a warrior leader. Moses was tolerant of behaviors that would eventually destroy the entire generation older than twenty years of age in the desert. Moses led the children of Israel out of Egypt but they failed in their wilderness to pass into the new season of being a blessed nation. They could not conquer their own fears of warfare and these fears opened their lives to behaviors that led to destructive sins. The New Testament warns us today to be careful that we do not fail in the same manner. Our identity needs to reflect God's desires for us in our moment of time.

The primary issue at hand in their failure was warfare. God took them out of one nation as slaves to make them a conquering victorious nation. The wilderness was where their identity was to be made. Are you ready to see yourself as one who is victorious and able to conquer? If you are, you need to be ready to overcome some of the same spiritual enemies they faced in their season of change. Times change and people change but the enemies we face are universal and timeless. God wants us to overcome these foes in our hour now.

When God changed leaders He changed the mantles. Moses responded to the people like a shepherd while Joshua led them like a general. There is always a place for the quiet shepherding of hurting people in every move of God; but this new move is not focused or led by the shepherd. Joshua warned the tribes that had flocks and wanted to stay on the safe side of the Jordon River that they had to make a commitment to their brothers that they were going to war in this new season. He warned them not to make a home where it was safe because this would ensure their failure. They had to march with the entire nation when it was time to fight. This shift and change that is going on is a shift to warfare. You may be a shepherd by nature and spiritual gifting but do not refuse to fight. David was a shepherd who knew when it was time to fight. Make a decision that you will follow God's generals into the spiritual battles of our time. This is your future that you are fighting to possess.

When it was time to cross over into the Promise Land God told Moses to send out leaders to spy out the land first. He selected one from every tribe with a total of twelve men. He wanted them to see what a splendid land it was. It was prosperous and fertile filled with houses and farms that they would possess. God always starts with leaders. Every wilderness will be evacuated by leaders first. If you are a leader you need to heed these principles closely. If you are not a leader I would encourage you to align with leaders who follow this prosperous plan. People will always follow a leader. Some of the most dangerous leaders are the ones who follow the voice of the masses rather than obeying the voice of God.

When the twelve leaders returned from spying out the land ten had a terrible report. It was a report that filled the hearts of the people with fear. They made a declaration to all the people that they would be swallowed up and killed if they crossed the Jordon River. They proclaimed a message of fear with their lips that they were like grasshoppers in the sight of the giant people who dwelt where God assigned them to go.

Numbers 13:32-33 (NASB)

[32] So they gave out to the sons of Israel a bad report of the land which they had spied out, saying, "The land through which we have gone, in spying it out, is a land that devours

its inhabitants; and all the people whom we saw in it are men of *great* size.

[33] "There also we saw the Nephilim (the sons of Anak are part of the Nephilim); and we became like grasshoppers in our own sight, and so we were in their sight."

Numbers 14:1-4 (NASB)

[1] Then all the congregation lifted up their voices and cried, and the people wept that night.

[2] All the sons of Israel grumbled against Moses and Aaron; and the whole congregation said to them, "Would that we had died in the land of Egypt! Or would that we had died in this wilderness!

[3] "Why is the Lord bringing us into this land, to fall by the sword? Our wives and our little ones will become plunder; would it not be better for us to return to Egypt?"

[4] So they said to one another, "Let us appoint a leader and return to Egypt."

The enemy can intimidate us so that our voice becomes a weapon against us instead of a weapon against him. Why did Moses allow the ten leaders to remain in leadership? When Moses failed to silence them he failed as a leader. The people looked up to these twelve and Moses did not remove them from a place of influence. Why did he tolerate a public meeting that grew so quickly out of hand? The leaders continued to spread fear to all the people at a time God had declared was right for them to be victorious. Your victory will not come at a time when things are easy. You need to decide you will fight for your families and your assignment. If you are spreading a bad report to yourself or those around you stop now before it gets out of hand! You will never leave the crisis season of life by being afraid to face your enemies. There were two who had a different spirit in them; Joshua and Caleb.

Numbers 14:6-9 (NASB)

[6] Joshua the son of Nun and Caleb the son of Jephunneh, of those who had spied out the land, tore their clothes;

[7] and they spoke to all the congregation of the sons of Israel, saying, "The land which we passed through to spy out is an exceedingly good land.

⁸ "If the Lord is pleased with us, then He will bring us into this land and give it to us—a land which flows with milk and honey.

⁹ "Only do not rebel against the Lord; and do not fear the people of the land, for they will be our prey. Their protection has been removed from them, and the Lord is with us; do not fear them."

Joshua and Caleb both entered into agreement with their assignment from the Lord. They heard the new word from heaven regarding their identity. They refused to buy into the bad report. They tried to quiet the crowd by making a decree of agreement with what God had originally spoken to them. They made a stand that could have cost them their lives but God intervened.

Numbers 14:10 (NASB)

¹⁰ But all the congregation said to stone them with stones. Then the glory of the Lord appeared in the tent of meeting to all the sons of Israel.

God will intervene and protect us when we step out in faith to fulfill His word over our life. It must have been difficult to be the last two speakers at that church meeting. Everyone was worked up and ready to walk out on God and they refused to change their message. This display of courage spared their lives. God made a decree that would settle this dispute.

Numbers 14:22-33 (NASB)

²² "Surely all the men who have seen My glory and My signs which I performed in Egypt and in the wilderness, yet have put Me to the test these ten times and have not listened to My voice,

²³ shall by no means see the land which I swore to their fathers, nor shall any of those who spurned Me see it.

²⁴ "But My servant Caleb, because he has had a different spirit and has followed Me fully, I will bring into the land which he entered, and his descendants shall take possession of it.

²⁵ "Now the Amalekites and the Canaanites live in the valleys; turn tomorrow and set out to the wilderness by the way of the

Red Sea."

²⁶ The Lord spoke to Moses and Aaron, saying,

²⁷ "How long *shall I bear* with this evil congregation who are grumbling against Me? I have heard the complaints of the sons of Israel, which they are making against Me.

²⁸ "Say to them, 'As I live,' says the Lord, 'just as you have spoken in My hearing, so I will surely do to you;

²⁹ your corpses will fall in this wilderness, even all your numbered men, according to your complete number from twenty years old and upward, who have grumbled against Me.

³⁰ 'Surely you shall not come into the land in which I swore to settle you, except Caleb the son of Jephunneh and Joshua the son of Nun.

³¹ 'Your children, however, whom you said would become a prey—I will bring them in, and they will know the land which you have rejected.

³² 'But as for you, your corpses will fall in this wilderness.

³³ 'Your sons shall be shepherds for forty years in the wilderness, and they will suffer *for* your unfaithfulness, until your corpses lie in the wilderness.

God took the murmuring and complaining of the people personally. He said they had an unfaithful spirit that would cause them to die in the wilderness. He said that Caleb and Joshua would live because they obeyed Him fully. They had a different spirit in them than the rest of the people. They were the ones the crowd would not have voted for as leaders. They were the ones that would have been stoned and killed because they dared to say that God can do the impossible. Our new identity under Jesus the General will give us faith and boldness that some will not understand or accept. In times of crisis there will always be the crowd looking to take a vote to go back instead of going forward. Who will you allow to speak into your life? The newspapers and television reporters would have told us that Joshua and Caleb were the bad guys in this moment. Who are you going to allow to tell you how to navigate your path out of the crisis?

This is all a part of spiritual warfare. Moses was praying when he should have been acting. He was comfortable with the role of a shepherd but it was time for him to embrace a new identity for the mission at hand.

He should have walked up and moved the unbelieving voices out of the camp before they were able to take control of the crowd. There is a time for prayer and there is a time to act. Make sure you are able to do both and have the wisdom to know God's timing. Take a moment right now and declare, "I will obey the voice of the Lord fully. I will shift in my identity as a soldier in God's army. Lord I enlist right now."

Chapter 8

Strategies for Your Season of Success

Carry His Presence

Joshua 1:5-9 (NASB)

[5] "No man will *be able to* stand before you all the days of your life. Just as I have been with Moses, I will be with you; I will not fail you or forsake you.

[6] "Be strong and courageous, for you shall give this people possession of the land which I swore to their fathers to give them.

[7] "Only be strong and very courageous; be careful to do according to all the law which Moses My servant commanded you; do not turn from it to the right or to the left, so that you may have success wherever you go.

[8] "This book of the law shall not depart from your mouth, but you shall meditate on it day and night, so that you may be careful to do according to all that is written in it; for then you will make your way prosperous, and then you will have success.

[9] "Have I not commanded you? Be strong and courageous! Do not tremble or be dismayed, for the Lord your God is with you wherever you go."

The stories of warfare under Joshua are extremely graphic and victorious. Something happened with that group in the wilderness that galvanized their hearts into a united warring nation. They were fearless of their enemies and fearful and obedient of their God. This is the attitude we must possess in order to move out of our crisis. The fearful and unbelieving may never get out of crisis but there will be a group who does. Make a declaration that you are going to be a part of the victorious people that will emerge. "I will be strong and courageous! The word of God will not depart from my mouth. The Lord my God will be with me wherever I go!"

Joshua led the people victoriously and miraculously across the Jordon River. This river crossing was much different from the Red Sea crossing. The Red Sea was a time of fearful prayers and groaning. It got so bad that God told Moses to stop crying and to take his rod of authority and tell the Red Sea to part. The crossing of the Jordon was totally different. It was a picture of order, discipline, faith and unity. Thank God for your Red Sea season but now declare that you are going to be a part of a new season and a new group of people. You are shifting from the season of the shepherd to the season of the General! Read how they crossed the Jordon…

Joshua 3:5-17 (NASB)

[5] Then Joshua said to the people, "Consecrate yourselves, for tomorrow the Lord will do wonders among you."

[6] And Joshua spoke to the priests, saying, "Take up the ark of the covenant and cross over ahead of the people." So they took up the ark of the covenant and went ahead of the people.

[7] Now the Lord said to Joshua, "This day I will begin to exalt you in the sight of all Israel, that they may know that just as I have been with Moses, I will be with you.

[8] "You shall, moreover, command the priests who are carrying the ark of the covenant, saying, 'When you come to the edge of the waters of the Jordan, you shall stand *still* in the Jordan.' "

[9] Then Joshua said to the sons of Israel, "Come here, and hear the words of the Lord your God."

[10] Joshua said, "By this you shall know that the living God is among you, and that He will assuredly dispossess from before you the Canaanite, the Hittite, the Hivite, the Perizzite, the Girgashite, the Amorite, and the Jebusite.

[11] "Behold, the ark of the covenant of the Lord of all the earth is crossing over ahead of you into the Jordan.

[12] "Now then, take for yourselves twelve men from the tribes of Israel, one man for each tribe.

[13] "It shall come about when the soles of the feet of the priests who carry the ark of the Lord, the Lord of all the earth, rest in the waters of the Jordan, the waters of the Jordan will be cut off, *and* the waters which are flowing down from above will stand in one heap."

[14] So when the people set out from their tents to cross the

Jordan with the priests carrying the ark of the covenant before the people,

¹⁵ and when those who carried the ark came into the Jordan, and the feet of the priests carrying the ark were dipped in the edge of the water (for the Jordan overflows all its banks all the days of harvest),

¹⁶ the waters which were flowing down from above stood *and* rose up in one heap, a great distance away at Adam, the city that is beside Zarethan; and those which were flowing down toward the sea of the Arabah, the Salt Sea, were completely cut off. So the people crossed opposite Jericho.

¹⁷ And the priests who carried the ark of the covenant of the Lord stood firm on dry ground in the middle of the Jordan while all Israel crossed on dry ground, until all the nation had finished crossing the Jordan.

The Ark represented the presence of the Lord. It was carried on the shoulders of the Priests. In the past God had one man, Moses that was able to release His authority over the Red Sea. This time God had a nation that released His Presence. Joshua had all of Moses' authority but something greater was now in the entire nation. They had become a nation of people carrying God's presence into the midst of a flooding river. The waters had to part for the will of God to be accomplished at this time. There may be a flood trying to stand between you and your destiny but this is the time to cross over into your new season with the people who carry God's presence into our modern world with its problems and needs.

This crossing was so much different than the Red Sea crossing. The Red Sea group ran through with fear and their enemies chasing them. God destroyed the enemies in a miraculous manner. This new group under Joshua's leadership was passing over the waters of the Jordon to chase down their enemies and destroy them with their own hands. This is a time to stop running from your enemies and become a part of a people that are going to destroy their enemies. This is God's plan for you now. This season of change will bring opportunities for you to see God create solutions to your problems with your own hands or actions. Daniel saw a great company of people who would do exploits for their God. This is the season for this group to emerge.

The Lord had established a priesthood that carried the Ark of the

Covenant into the Jordon River. This new season that God is creating is a season that will be different than what you have experienced in the past. God is connecting us together, or aligning us in such a way that we are going to see a new parting of the waters that stand in our way. This is a season of being properly aligned. Who are you submitted to follow? Who can speak into your life? Is there someone that can tell you honest things you don't want to hear? Are you willing to stay and submit rather than bouncing from group to group when you get your feelings hurt? There is going to be a priesthood that carries His presence! This group is aligned under the General.

Get connected and stay connected. Your moments to be offended are just opportunities to repent and get well. If you take care of yourself God will take care of the rest. Look inward before looking at others. Talk to God about yourself before you to talk about someone else! This is an hour when God is cleansing His temple. When we think it is all about us or our gift and our anointing we are missing the point. God has to clean this selfish thinking up. Every time you think someone has done something wrong to you ask God to reveal to you your true motives and why you are offended. You will find that most of the time your offense will have nothing to do with the person you are mad at right now.

I see this as a time that people are going to have great advances over past offences. What used to take several weeks of counseling can be removed in moments or hours in His presence. The deepest wounds can have the arrows of poison removed by the presence of our Holy God. This is only true for those who refuse to take up weapons against their fellow man. This is not the time to create factions among the people with your opinions. Declare I am not going to get into a fight with my brother or sister in Christ. I am going to get healed of my past wounds and hurts. I will be victorious. I will be properly connected!

People of presence know how to be thankful for what they have rather than grumbling about what they don't. People who create an environment for God's manifest presence know how to ask God to forgive them if they do anything to hinder Him in our midst. This is a season to have a greater sensitivity to what grieves the Holy Spirit. This is the group that will see the waters part as we move into our future and our destiny. God is calling you to this united priesthood that ushers in His presence.

Everyone had to step into the river before the waters parted. You may want the waters to part before you step forward; or you may want everything to be finished before you start; it doesn't work this way. You have to make a decision to be hungry for the presence of God above any gifts from God. You need to long for Him more than for what He can do for you. Make a decision that the holy and righteous presence of God is a priority to you.

Once the priests stepped into the river the rest of the nation followed. Most people would like to see God touch the government, the schools and the marketplace. We are quick to see someone else that needs the presence of God to heal and change them, but God is starting with those who call themselves Christians. We are the ones that need to step into God's healing river first. Once we do, the others that come behind us will pass through as well.

Rivers create divides in the natural. There are banks on both sides and neither side is able to connect to the other. The troubles swirling in the world are creating great divisions with strong emotions of resistance towards anyone not on the same side. Christians are not immune from entering into this strong emotional pool of toxic emotions. Some will even say that their bitterness and anger is of the Lord. This is not the Lord. Even when God is angry with sin or behavior He has a redemptive message of faith, hope and love. Don't be left on the banks of division in this season.

The only safe place from division in this new season we are approaching is in the river of God. The river of His presence is not a cute saying or a time of frivolous fun. It is really a determination to seek God and walk with Him. To know what the Father is doing and being a part of it. The river of God is bringing healing to all the nations as it flows out from God's temple. We are that temple and the river should be flowing out of our inner most being. When you choose to live your life in God's river you will see your life improve. Refuse to be an observer of the river and determine to be immersed in the river.

Using analogies and modern words are not meant to be confusing.

There is a place we can be at in our life where God's Spirit is so real and clear to us that He is able to lead us like we are in a boat floating in a river. Our attitudes, emotions and constant thought life can hinder this process. It is possible to live in the earth with a life that is so connected to God that we are directed by Him continually. This is becoming more readily apparent now than in times past. There used to be some people that could tap into this intimate relationship with God; now He is raising up an entire people group to walk this way.

When you move into this level of fellowship in the Holy Spirit you will recognize others who are walking like this with God when you meet them. There is an inner peace that creates peace for others around them. There is a joy that is not silly but it releases encouragement and hope to those who are in contact with them. They have a sense of God's acceptance and love that makes others feel the same way. All of these explanations are what I mean when I say that we need to step into the river to avoid the schism of division in the world.

Jesus was like this. He had the ability to make everyone around Him feel accepted and loved. Even people that were controlled by demons had the emotional capacity to fall at His feet and ask for help. He carried the presence of God's kingdom with Him in the emotional realm that emitted from Him. The ones who did not like Him or like to be around Him were the people that were filled with their own thoughts and opinions about God. These were the religious people that ruled over everyone. Jesus challenged them for wanting to be important while never doing anything to help others get better. Jesus represents the ultimate priest who stepped into the river. He wants us to be like Him while we are on the earth. This is not sinless perfection but it is awareness and quick repentance when we do sin.

We are entering into a new season of harvest in the earth. The people of faith all around the world are being called to join together to step forward with one voice and one purpose. This is to glorify God and show others what the kingdom is like. There will be a group of people that are diversified and different on the outside but they all look like Jesus on the inside. These are the ones who are coming out of the wilderness at this time. They will emerge through the river and under the direction of their General.

There is a tangible awareness of God's heart when you get off the banks of division and into the river of His Presence. This might sound strange to some of you but it is a reality that will change your life. I have met so many people that have come into my life because of God's manifest presence when I minister. The testimonies have a powerful common thread. They have been forever changed by the presence of God. If you need this type of change in your heart and soul ask Him to reveal His presence to you even now. Stop reading and wait on God to touch your heart in a way you have never been touched before. This will get you off the banks of division and into a place of healing. God wants you to find peace more than you do. He is here right now next to you. Step into the river.

The Priest stepped into the river at the time of harvest. You are entering into a season of harvest. What will the crop you harvest look like? Will you continue to harvest pain and suffering or will you harvest a new life and new emotions? You can; all this is available to you right now. Every person has a physical network of synapses in their brain. Medical tests have shown that when we focus on something long enough we create the electrical currents and pathways necessary to achieve what we have focused upon. This is why some people are addicted to unrighteous thoughts and behaviors. The thoughts stayed in their mind long enough to get the wires or synapses firing in a way to make them a slave to sin. If you stay in this place you will harvest more unrighteousness. It is time to start dwelling or meditating upon the promises of God.

This is how you will see a change. Change your environments from darkness to light. Are there places you go that create emotions and feelings that are negative? Get out of those places and don't go back. Are there places you go that create positive emotions? Go to these places more often. Engage yourself in the activities that will move you into your new season of friends, behaviors thoughts and actions.

There are words that God is speaking to you that can rewire your brain and emotional pathways. You need to step into your new identity in this new season. The old identity is not who you are. Even if it was yesterday, it does not need to be who you are today! Your old friends might condemn you. Even your own heart or mind might condemn you. I tell you if you fix your thoughts on what God is saying about you a new identity will emerge.

Step into your new identity right now. Declare that you are holy, righteous and forgiven. You are not a slave to sin or unrighteousness. You are a priest of the Most High God! You are a part of a group of people that are going to emerge victoriously in this new season. Ask the Holy Spirit to fill any sick or hurting areas of your brain or your heart with His healing presence right now. Soak in this presence and allow new pathways to be formed in your physical body. You are stepping into the river and there is a harvest of a new identity in Christ waiting to be formed in you. You will be a part of the victorious people who are under the leadership of Jesus our General.

Possess the Possible

The season of change was upon Joshua and all the people. They were radically different from the ones who lived in the wilderness for forty years. They did not focus on what they could not do. They went out ready to possess the possible! This is what it should be like for all of us who serve the living God. We should look notably different when we come out of the wilderness. People that have not seen you in a year will be amazed at what you look like, talk like and act like when they get around you. Are you comfortable being so changed that everyone is talking about you when you are not around? It is something that will allow God's glory to touch them. When a person sees someone who has actually passed through the wilderness into a new season of victory it stays with them. I recently blessed the child born to a barren couple of seven years. The look on their faces was priceless. They are no longer barren and the presence of God was the source of their new season. I know that everyone who knows this couple will feel God's presence when they tell the story.

It was time for Joshua to lead the people against Jericho; a strong walled city that seemed to be impenetrable. It was described as being well fortified. It was in the land that the twelve spies forty years earlier had traversed and returned to Moses with a report of doom and gloom. This time Joshua sent out two spies not twelve. They moved into a covert mission to see what they were up against but not with the eyes of fear, with the expectations of faith. The report that came back was far different than the first one…

Joshua 2:23-24 (NASB)

[23] Then the two men returned and came down from the hill country and crossed over and came to Joshua the son of Nun, and they related to him all that had happened to them.

[24] They said to Joshua, "Surely the Lord has given all the land into our hands; moreover, all the inhabitants of the land have melted away before us."

The two men returned and gave a very simple strait forward response to Joshua. The Lord has given the land into our hands and the inhabitants have melted away before us. What a difference in the voice and the mindset of these men. This is the same difference that you are now becoming. You are no longer living in your wilderness. As you are going through this book and applying what is being released you are moving out and moving into your new season. Your new season is not one with the absence of problems. It is a season to conquer our problems with a faith and belief that every assignment from God will be given into our hands.

In the Matrix Trilogy movies we see a very powerful fiction story about what is real and what is perceived. The story revolves around a small group of people who refuse to be deceived by the matrix that shows the world as one way to the masses but when they are not plugged into the matrix they can see what is actually happening. The enemy has a matrix on our minds that he is so powerful and cunning that we could never defeat him. In reality, he and his forces are melting away in fear that we will one day be free from his deceptive matrix. He fears the people that will emerge from this wilderness crisis with a clear view of what the Lord is about to deliver into their hands.

As you emerge from your wilderness your eyes will be fixed on the prize that the Lord wants you to possess. It no longer seems like something impossible. Possessing the possible is a matter of fact. God is going to do it and the enemy is going to fall. We are becoming like these two men who returned to Joshua with a good report. God is going to give it to us and our enemy is afraid of our nation of priests armed with His presence.

What is your Jericho? What has been a walled city that you could not penetrate in the past? What have you never dared to believe God could do in your life? When you leave your crisis you are entering into a new time and purpose. You are not leaving your crisis to sit around and watch television. You are not leaving to have a life of ease. You are going to be connected to a group of people that are advancing God's kingdom into realms of darkness that have not been penetrated. You are not going to advance alone; you are going with a team of trained and empowered people. You are now a part of the apostolos of God shifting culture and influence with His Presence.

Jericho is in your assignment but it is not your final destination. Jericho was the first city but it was not the last. You are about to enter into a new season of progressive victories. You need a plan and a strategy to see these walled fortresses come down. This is where you are going to start applying all the concepts you have learned in this book. You will connect with prophetic and apostolic intercessors to see the walls of deception and control broken. God will invade these fortified cities with His manifest presence.

Chapter 9

Giving Out of Crisis

First Fruits: Always Give the First and the Best

Jericho was a First Fruits city. God instituted a principle with Joshua and the people called First Fruits. This was taught to them while they were in the wilderness but it was not put into practice until they crossed the Jordon and passed into the Promise Land. This is a principle we must get right in our hearts as we move out of our wilderness and crisis and move into a new season of life.

First Fruits is simply giving God the first and the best of something as an act of faith. We believe there is more to come after it. Jericho was the first city to fall and God said that the first part is always holy for Him. When we sanctify the first, the rest that comes later is holy as well.

> **Joshua 6:17-19 (NASB)**
> [17] "The city shall be under the ban, it and all that is in it belongs to the Lord; only Rahab the harlot and all who are with her in the house shall live, because she hid the messengers whom we sent.
> [18] "But as for you, only keep yourselves from the things under the ban, so that you do not covet *them* and take some of the things under the ban, and make the camp of Israel accursed and bring trouble on it.
> [19] "But all the silver and gold and articles of bronze and iron are holy to the Lord; they shall go into the treasury of the Lord."

First Fruits is a Promise Land principle. Everyone planning on moving out of the crisis and into success needs to understand that God is serious about this offering. God commanded that all the silver and gold from the first city go into the treasury of the Lord. The principle of first fruits breaks the stronghold of covetousness from our life. The Lord wants us to be disciplined in a way that allows us to see wealth, increase and prosperity in a godly light. There is a kingdom purpose for wealth. Wealth and the spoils of success are not for our wasteful pleasures. When you practice first fruits you are expressing a discipline that will protect your heart from evil.

Practical expressions of first fruits can come in different ways. The most important step in this offering is hearing from the Lord. Joshua heard that all the gold and silver belonged to the Lord. This was not written in the law. It was a word for that moment. This is what makes this offering special and difficult at the same time. Some people want to know the formula so they can be obedient. They want someone else to put the formula out there rather than seeking God for the right amount. I can help you understand the principle but I am challenging you to learn to hear from God.

When you navigate out of your crisis you may be reformed into a new place of career employment. This might be your dream job or it might be a stepping stone towards something different. No matter, the first portion of finances from this new job belongs to God. How much should you give? The first month's, week's, or day's wages could be a good place to start to consider. Pray and ask God to tell you and then give it with a joyful heart.

You are learning something very important about yourself and about God. You are honoring God with the best portion of the first. You trust Him to have more of this continuing to come in. The gift is voluntary but it should be significant. More than the ten percent tithe. What if you are doing contract labor? You might devote the first contract to God entirely and then you start to tithe ten percent of the rest of the jobs that come afterwards. It is up to you, but once you pass out of the wilderness you need to get this principle down in your heart and don't forget to practice it. If you get an unexpected gift or bonus give first fruits from that gift rather than tithing. Think of it as God's opportunity for abundance to come into your life. When you give first fruits from these unexpected or rarely seen sources of income, you are opening the door for more of them to come your way!

Israel had complete favor and they had no difficulty overcoming the strong walled city of Jericho. They all obeyed the Lord concerning first fruits with the exception of one family. This one family's disobedience cost several men's lives when Israel went up against the next city of Ai. Joshua fell on his face before God and wanted to know why they did not have the same success as they did in Jericho. God answered him with these words...

Joshua 7:13 (NASB)

[13] "Rise up! Consecrate the people and say, 'Consecrate yourselves for tomorrow, for thus the Lord, the God of Israel, has said, "There are things under the ban in your midst, O Israel. You cannot stand before your enemies until you have removed the things under the ban from your midst."

The second blessing of first fruits is found in this statement. We are able to stand against our enemies that are withstanding us when we fully give our first fruits. Once it was known what God wanted as a first fruits offering from Jericho, everyone was expected to obey fully. When you and your family give first fruits offerings to God you need to make sure that everyone is equally committed.

When we think about this on a larger scale it is both amazing and scary. What would happen to our success rate if all the people emerging from this time of wilderness crisis practiced full obedience in the realm of first fruits? This goes back to our word on this being a season of alignment. There would be such tremendous spiritual victories we would be amazed. We need to be in agreement with people who have the same values. This new generation under Joshua's leadership was not fickle and independent. They were committed and united at a corporate level of obedience that released corporate victories. We must use the strategies of first fruits as a tool of warfare as we move into our future.

Sanctify the Righteous Seeds

Inside of every person is a righteous seed planted by God when He created them. Inside of each one of us are spiritual gifts created to glorify God. The most powerful king that Joshua would face was a king who had his god given talents turned against God's purposes. This is found in the story of the five Amorite kings who went to war against Gibeon because Gibeon had submitted to Joshua. They hated anyone who would submit to God. This story reveals to us how the enemy can take something that is created to be holy and it becomes a tool in his hand.

When Joshua and the people of Israel crossed the Jordon they began to see God move in new and exciting ways. He continued to reveal Himself to them with strategies for every city. They obeyed the Lord and they saw each city fall before them. Things were prospering as they left the wilderness and entered into their new identity as a nation. When they started to prosper the enemy created an unholy alliance or a force multiplier to defeat God's people. It would be the most devious attack yet in the Promise Land.

This is where many people have been before. There are those who have had a measure of success and feel that they are not in a crisis or a wilderness. They have moved forward but after a while they are stalled out because of a warfare they had not encountered before or are not able to stand against. This attack uses God given gifts and talents against us because they are unredeemed and not sanctified. Things that have an origin in God are activated by the enemy to trap us and keep us from the fulfillment of our destiny.

Some will come very close to the prize and then it is snatched away before it is theirs. It is like a false pregnancy; everything looks real but there is no fruit. Over time hope deferred creates sadness and faith is ultimately robbed. How can this be? Somewhere in your life the enemy has turned a seed designed by God to make you successful as a tool against you. The enemy we face is very deceptive in this way. We can live a lifetime and never realize why we continually failed to remain victorious.

Joshua 10:1-5 (NASB)
[1] Now it came about when Adoni-zedek king of Jerusalem heard that Joshua had captured Ai, and had utterly destroyed it (just as he had done to Jericho and its king, so he had done to Ai and its king), and that the inhabitants of Gibeon had made peace with Israel and were within their land,
[2] that he feared greatly, because Gibeon *was* a great city, like one of the royal cities, and because it was greater than Ai, and all its men *were* mighty.
[3] Therefore Adoni-zedek king of Jerusalem sent *word* to

Hoham king of Hebron and to Piram king of Jarmuth and to Japhia king of Lachish and to Debir king of Eglon, saying,
⁴"Come up to me and help me, and let us attack Gibeon, for it has made peace with Joshua and with the sons of Israel."
⁵ So the five kings of the Amorites, the king of Jerusalem, the king of Hebron, the king of Jarmuth, the king of Lachish, *and* the king of Eglon, gathered together and went up, they with all their armies, and camped by Gibeon and fought against it.

When studying the name of the first king we see that he is an ungodly king who possesses a godly name in his origin. Adoni-zedek means, Lord of righteousness, and king of peace. Why would someone with this name want to fight against the armies of God? He was afraid of being conquered. He must always be the one in control. He will use everything he can get his hands on to stop his circumstances from making him vulnerable to the will and desires of someone else. The most deadly opponents we will face are those areas of our life that God created for good, but the flesh has corrupted it for evil. In this hour of alignment this king is going to try and stop God's people from gaining momentum and taking the mountains of cultural influence. He will work with people who are against the faith and those within the faith. This king is to be dealt with along our path after we have experienced measures of breakthrough and success. When we think we have it going on, watch out, he is coming up.

The enemy manifests the opposite fruit of what God created the gift to accomplish. One example could be the gift of leadership. Can you think of people that are really gifted at leading but it is not used for righteousness? They are out there right now and the power of the unsanctified God given gift is mobilizing people for unrighteous causes. Gang leaders, prison ring leaders, mafia bosses and more are all examples of people who are empowered by the gift of leadership that have never been redeemed in their life.

Another gift or trait is steadfastness. We use this word as a positive godly character in someone's life. It takes perseverance to stand up against the attacks and assaults that try to wear us down in our journey towards destiny. Those who refuse to wilt under pressure are a stalwart of encouragement to others around them. They will others to continue in the battle and not lose faith. What if this is not used in the right way?

If this character trait is not redeemed we call them stubborn. Some can be so stubborn they hinder the advancement of righteousness. Some are so stubborn they keep their entire family in darkness. Some are so stubborn they can stop the progress of entire communities. When we are facing an unredeemed character trait we are in for a different type of battle.

Lucifer believed in God and was in charge of a large ministry team of angels. Everything created in him by God is now used against God. We may think that only bad people have this problem but it is a battle every person will face. The devil will try to get us to use our spiritual DNA against the will of God rather than for it. This area of battle includes those who believe in Jesus and know that they have spiritual gifts. They think that they are doing God a favor by persecuting the church. This is what Saul of Tarsus was doing when the early church was prospering and advancing. Saul led the charge to shut it down. This demonic spirit will try to stop the momentum of God in His people. He will recruit other spirits and join forces to try and turn the move of God into a moment of God.

Hoham is a name that means to compromise. Compromise can sound like a good thing and tolerance might sound even better to some. What we tolerate we will manifest. When we decide that God's ways are not always the best ways we are going to be left alone because God does not tolerate compromise. There is room for God's love and mercy for people but not for sin. When the new season of God begins to start moving the subtlety of compromise will be a challenge. How much can we put up with and still see the manifest presence of God? Once you start thinking like that you will have already lost the manifest presence of God. He is holy and will not share His glory or His people with any other idol.

Piram was a king whose name comes from root words meaning a wild donkey. It is more than a rebellious animal; it refers to one that runs wild in the desert in a time of reproductive heat that causes others to chase after it. This is the season that true appointed leaders need to watch those with leadership gifts that are pushing to emerge before they are ready. They don't want to submit or wait for the timing of God. They want others to follow them now. There are people who lack discernment who will follow them because they have a gift. This type of leader will divert the people from the river of God. The joy and the momentum will be lost when people are pushing for positions.

Japhia was another king whose name means to shine. Again we see that this is a godly trait. This is a trait that attracts others. We are to shine to draw others to Jesus. When this is un-redeemed we see it drawing attention to our self. We have to guard against wanting to shine so others will watch us. Wanting to shine with the wrong motives brings a completely different spirit into the room. This is a season we are called to change atmospheres. You can see people who shine but can you discern the spirit that is being emitted? This is a move of God's presence and we must be discerning when people want to shine and the manifest presence begins to lift or leave.

Debir was the name of the last king. His name has roots of dealing with speech or legal matters. It also is connected with whispering or slander. The gift of speech is to build up and edify others. It can quickly be turned to start fires with whispers and slander. Watch out for this to turn during a time of godly momentum. One who was useful can be hurt and turn into one who begins to whisper. The change is subtle and deceptive to both the one speaking and the one who is listening. Jesus was always in conflict with legalistic leaders who loved to hear their own voice. They also were constrained by their methods. Legalism will follow whispering. It causes people stop moving and start judging one another. This is a trap to stop the move of God. Everyone in the camp of God needs to be responsible to stop the whisperers.

Fear of submission is at the root of all of this. Fear of not being in control will bring about the strongest battles we will ever face. When someone is refusing to submit to God they will create an unholy alliance to destroy those that want to submit to God. This is the unseen battle that takes too many Christians captive. In their quest to obey and submit to God they encounter demonic coalitions that network together to wear down the saints until they quit following their assignment. These unholy spirits will wear some down until they even begin to use their own spiritual DNA against their own self.

The sweetest little old saint that everyone loves and tolerates can be controlled by this unholy king Adoni-zedek and his alliance. How many pastors have left the ministry because of a supposedly peaceful righteous person in the local church? Whole congregations and denominations are shipwrecked from their destiny because of this king. This spirit has resisted the moves of God in the past and succeeded. It is going to take apostolic leadership to say you will not stop the move of God! Apostles, prophets, intercessors and all the saints must align together and not be deceived by the outside appearance that this principality masquerades behind. This ungodly king is at work right now trying to stop us from uniting and manifesting God's presence. Stop right now. Are you battling against others in the Body of Christ? Do you think that your cause is righteous? Are you willing to submit your cause to a higher authority and allow them to speak into your life? If not, you are being attacked by this self righteous peace robbing king. Declare, I will over come Adoni-zedek. I will remove the enemy from my spiritual gifts and eternal purpose. I will not align with evil, I submit to Jesus!

Chapter 10

Praying through the Crisis

Prophetic Intercession

As we move forward with our assignment we are going to face spiritual battles. This is going to require us to pray. How we pray is very important. There are prayers of petition which most people understand and practice. There are also prayers of proclamation which is a biblical method of prayer but not as well known at this point. During this shift from one season to another we must learn how to embrace and practice prayers of decree and proclamation. We need to understand the importance and how to practice prophetic intercession.

When we enter into prophetic intercession we are speaking what God says over a situation, a person, or a nation. Petition is asking God for something. Most people are more comfortable with petition or asking. The problem is when we are asking for things God has already said He would do we are not going to move forward in our destiny. There is an enemy creating problems in our pathway to destiny that requires a different type of prayer to be evicted. It is time for us to shift in our mind and method regarding how we pray. Prophetic declarations are important in this time of moving from one season to another. God is changing you from one form to another. How you pray needs to change now in order to leave your wilderness and embrace your new season.

The religious spirit resists change. It does not want us to be the empowered people of God. It affects the way that we pray. It may cause us to question, who am I to make a declaration or proclamation? God wants us to make proclamations. A proclamation is to officially announce what the king or person in authority has already said to be made known publically. Prophetic proclamations can be released by reading the scriptures out loud. In this way you are saying what God said!

Combining our assignment with our proclamation is the most affective way to see prayers of declaration fulfilled. Timing is a very important variable. Many places in scripture reference the timing of God to be correct for a certain event to occur. People in the days of the Old Testament could have declared a virgin would give birth, but it was Mary's assignment when the fullness of time came to pass. When the angel came and declared the will of God to Mary, she did not give a prayer of petition asking, "If it be thy will let it be done." No she entered into agreement with what God had said and her assignment to fulfill the event. She declared, "Behold the bondslave of the Lord. Let it be done according to His word." When we sense that we are in the right timing for something to come to pass and it is biblical, we need to release the decree with faith.

Prophetic words and decrees are essential in having success with the spiritual battles you will face. Your faith is connected to what has been spoken over you and to you. You cannot win a spiritual battle without faith. The very essence of spiritual warfare is you dealing with the powers of the unseen yet truly felt and experienced forces of darkness.

I have written much about the prophetic in this book. I know for some of you this is something that you might not be personally experiencing or know how to identify. I want to make this as simple as possible because you must embrace the prophetic and become a prophetic person to advance through your warfare.

Have you ever had a thought that could have come from God about something you are supposed to do? I mean, it is not illegal or immoral, or outside of the biblical boundaries, but it takes faith to believe that it could really happen. This is an example of how a prophetic moment can enter your life. The scriptures show that people say prophetic things to each other even when they may not be aware of it.

Another aspect of a prophetic word is that it bears witness or strikes a chord of truth in your own heart when you hear it. This also needs to be in agreement with the biblical standards. Something is said and you know in your heart that you are connected to this statement. Somehow it was said so it would prompt you into some type of action. What are you supposed to do with it?

There are four steps in how God fulfills His will with us on the earth. The first is a promise. The promise is prophetic in nature because it is not a reality right now. Every great event, structure, civilization, etc started with a promise or a vision in someone's heart. The promise is connected to your destiny and it requires both faith and action on your part. This promise is able to motivate you into your assignment no matter what is standing in your way.

This leads to the second step; the problem. God knew that the problem was coming and He needed to get your motivation in action. Some think that if God really wants something to happen there will not be any problems. This is not true. In reality, the things in life of greatest value are the most difficult to achieve. It does not take faith to be unemployed or addicted to a substance. Changing our world and the world of others around us will always have obstacles in the way. The greater the promise the greater the problem is a true saying. Don't give up on your dreams or promises or the prophetic just because things are difficult.

The third step is the process of God. This is how God takes you on a journey and teaches you how to embrace His principles for life over the principles of death and destruction. Some people take years to learn the process. In reality, the process can be compared to the wilderness season of your life. In the wilderness you are going to be alone to be spoken to by the Lord. When you get that word you will know how to obey to move forward into your next season. This is a process that God uses to cause us to mature to have the capacity and ability to be successful in our new season of life that He had promised.

The final step is the provision of God. What was promised becomes a reality as we overcome the problems with the tools gained in the process. This all sounds simple but in reality we might go through this cycle three or four times in a lifetime before we actually reach our destiny and ultimate assignment from God. Some people get lost in this wilderness experience and they are overcome by their problems and the negative thoughts connected to them and they quit. They don't experience their destiny because they did not know how to get out of the wilderness.

This is why this Chapter on spiritual warfare is so important. The bible is filled with examples of warfare. The Old Testament tells historical stories and the New Testament tells us that we battle with invisible forces of evil. This is not fiction it is reality. Those who refuse to fight for their promises will be lost in the problems they face in this world. Most that choose this path have a belief system that blames God for not doing His part. This cannot be you in this hour. You need to know how God wants to work through you and with you. This is the only way He can work for you!

Part of the process that we must embrace before we see our promises fulfilled, our wilderness end, and our destiny embraced is to learn how to engage in spiritual warfare. The Apostle Paul had a promising leader under his training that he had assigned to lead in a city. This young man was sent with a promise but was facing great opposition. Paul instructed him to engage in spiritual warfare using prophesies or promises spoken to him...

1 Timothy 1:18-19 (NASB)
[18] This command I entrust to you, Timothy, *my* son, in accordance with the prophecies previously made concerning you, that by them you fight the good fight,
[19] keeping faith and a good conscience, which some have rejected and suffered shipwreck in regard to their faith.

Our promise of destiny is prophetic in nature. It starts us on a journey that will be filled with opposition. The devil is going to do everything in his power to influence people and situations to discourage you before you reach your destiny. Some will be shipwrecked in their journey because they refused to fight this fight of faith. Timothy was instructed to use the prophetic promise made over his life to wage war against the enemy. We must do the same. You are going to have to speak up and out loud that God has spoken a promise to you that nothing is going to stop. Write down your promises and pray over them until they become a reality. Don't simply wait for them to happen one day, because that day might not come without you praying it through.

The problems Timothy continued experiencing with people became very difficult. They thought he was too young to lead them and they were not following his leadership. Look at the strategy the Apostle Paul gave his young friend...

1 Timothy 4:14-16 (NASB)

[14] Do not neglect the spiritual gift within you, which was bestowed on you through prophetic utterance with the laying on of hands by the presbytery.

[15] Take pains with these things; be *absorbed* in them, so that your progress will be evident to all.

[16] Pay close attention to yourself and to your teaching; persevere in these things, for as you do this you will ensure salvation both for yourself and for those who hear you.

Can you see the four principles I have just written about? Paul reminds Timothy that the spiritual gift in his life was given to him by the Lord when someone spoke a prophetic word over his life. The supernatural gift that God placed in Timothy to be successful and to make others successful was released when someone spoke a creative word of God over him. He now needed to grow in the process of developing that gift so he and the others would benefit by him moving into his destiny.

Here is another word of encouragement from Paul to Timothy a little later…

2 Timothy 1:5-7 (NASB)

[5] For I am mindful of the sincere faith within you, which first dwelt in your grandmother Lois and your mother Eunice, and I am sure that *it is* in you as well.

[6] For this reason I remind you to kindle afresh the gift of God which is in you through the laying on of my hands.

[7] For God has not given us a spirit of timidity, but of power and love and discipline.

Paul was reminding Timothy again about the gift of faith that he had to put to work. He used Timothy's mom and grandmother as examples of how to persevere through difficulty with this gift of faith. He had to overcome the fear that was trying to stop him while he was in his wilderness. God was not the source of him becoming afraid or timid. God is the true source of the discipline we need to overcome our fears. He gives us the perfect love in our hearts to cast out all fear. We have the authority and power to overcome the obstacles in our life and break out of the wilderness! Take a moment right now and say, "I am not fearful! I have God's love and authority to overcome my troubles!"

We have to believe in our hearts that what we do with prayer really matters. We must decree both the written scriptures and the principles of the written scriptures. When God prompts something in our hearts for this hour we need to decide if it aligns with the principles of scripture. When it does, we have to change these thoughts into our words to fight against spiritual evil. Look at this scripture.

2 Corinthians 10:2-6 (NKJV)

[2] But I beg *you* that when I am present I may not be bold with that confidence by which I intend to be bold against some, who think of us as if we walked according to the flesh.
[3] For though we walk in the flesh, we do not war according to the flesh.
[4] For the weapons of our warfare *are* not carnal but mighty in God for pulling down strongholds,
[5] casting down arguments and every high thing that exalts itself against the knowledge of God, bringing every thought into captivity to the obedience of Christ,
[6] and being ready to punish all disobedience when your obedience is fulfilled.

What are the divinely empowered weapons that are spoken about in this passage of scripture? The weapons are literally the verbal prayers, declarations and acts of obedience to God. Something supernatural is released in the unseen realms when we do all the above. This is why we must overcome our natural or carnal mind that wants us to be so analytical that we never engage in active prayer.

There is a connection between our earthly obedience and the punishment of the evil that is disobedient to the ways of God. We are told to cast down every argument and high thing that exalts itself against the knowledge of God. This means I need to take my personal thoughts captive. I cannot allow my mind and imagination to run wild with thoughts that will get me emotionally charged to sin against the principles of God.

It also means that I need to make a declaration with my voice that these powers are not going to destroy my family, my city, or my nation. I cannot simply sit in silence thinking that as long as I am not doing something wrong it does not apply to me. Think about this in the natural. You may not be a policeman but if someone is breaking into your neighbor's house you will use your voice to declare to the authorities a violation of law is in progress. What would your neighbor say if you told him a week later you saw someone breaking in and stealing his possession but you remained silent and disengaged? We are responsible to be the eyes and ears of authority and declare righteousness.

When we are engaged in spiritual battles we must report illegal activity that is outside of the boundaries of God's laws or principles for man. Some do this by telling their pastor what they see and perceive to be wrong. He has a voice but so do you! You need to become involved. When we see it and declare God's judgment upon it, it releases His creative power to stop the work of the devil.

Decrees are governmental. God releases His authority and His power into the earth through His voice; this is the primary way that God releases His authority. When God wants to create, judge, or release the miraculous, much of this is done through His voice. We are the voice of the Lord in the earth. His Spirit is now living inside of you. The power of life and death are in the tongue! When God wants to release that power and authority we become His spokespersons in the earth. Sometimes we ask, but most of the time we declare it.

Isaiah 55:11; Jeremiah 1:12 and Job 22:27-28 are all examples of what God has spoken about Himself, His word and His promises and us. As you read these remember that everything He is saying about Himself is actually going to come to pass through a person who spoke and wrote these words down…

Isaiah 55:11 (NASB)
[11] So will My word be which goes forth from My mouth; It will not return to Me empty, Without accomplishing what I desire, And without succeeding *in the matter* for which I sent it.

Jeremiah 1:12 (NASB)
[12] Then the Lord said to me, "You have seen well, for I am watching over My word to perform it."

Job 22:27-28 (NASB)

[27] You will pray to Him, and He will hear you;
And you will pay your vows,
[28] You will also decree a thing, and it will be established
for you; And light will shine on your ways

These scriptures are words that were spoken through people. God did not simply speak out of the heavens where man could hear Him. He spoke through people that sensed what He was saying into their hearts and then they released it to others and even wrote what God said down. When the person on earth was obedient to speak it out loud, God then performed what was said on the earth. Everything God said to the prophets He was able to do.

When God says that His word will perform, or accomplish in these different passages they are forms of the Hebrew word which means to do or to make. It is one of the two words used in Genesis to describe how God made the earth. It shows us that God uses this creative power for various purposes in the earth continually after the initial creation. God's word has life and our words have life!

Proverbs 18:21 (NASB)

[21] Death and life are in the power of the tongue, And those who love it will eat its fruit.

Our words have creative power for our future. We can declare life with what we say or we can declare death. This is how God has made us and this is why our words are essential in our spiritual warfare. Our words are also connected to the work and world of the angelic hosts…

Psalms 103:20 (NASB)

[20] Bless the Lord, you His angels, Mighty in strength, who perform His word, Obeying the voice of His word!

When we release prophetic proclamations in our prayers we are releasing the angels of God to perform that specific word. Angels are assigned to help the heirs of salvation. We are the heirs of salvation. How do they help us? They help us in fulfilling our scriptural destiny.

When we pray or declare the scriptures over our life or life situations angels are released to start working in the unseen realms to assist in making new realities in the earth.

There are angels who have been waiting for centuries for the church to take on this new way of prayer. They are excited to work with us like they did with Jacob or Daniel. When you pray and make decrees agree with God and loose the angelic hosts to perform God's word on your behalf. They have an assignment just like we do. They are waiting on us before they do their job. Release a declaration over your life right now. *Father I thank you for the angelic hosts assigned to assist me in my assignment. I enter into agreement with them to work in the invisible realms to break the spiritual darkness I am facing. (Name the darkness). I decree that God's word, (Name the promise of scripture) is going to be a reality in my life and I will experience it in the Name of Jesus.* Now thank the Lord for releasing the angelic help you need for victory in this new season.

Prayers That Will Release Your Future

The great news about the shift of season that emerged with Joshua and his nation was they were victorious over the five kings. The strategy that had worked against others did not work against them. They had a unity and a resolve that would not break their love and devotion to God. They were willing to unite for the purpose of God's destiny above their own comforts or desires. They gave the first and the best to God and it opened up the gates of supply for their inheritance. They refused to be divided and they could not be defeated. This group of people made it from the desert into their destiny. They experienced the transfer of wealth because they knew their assignment and they would not be deterred from accomplishing it. They glorified God and made Him known to all the other nations around them. They moved across the river, brought forth God's presence, gained cities, gained momentum and in the end the last strategy to stop them failed. This is the example we need to embrace because this is where the church is at right now. Are you ready to be a part of the next victorious generation? I hope so because it is about to get better.

Joshua 10:16-25 (NASB)
[16] Now these five kings had fled and hidden themselves in the

cave at Makkedah.

¹⁷ It was told Joshua, saying, "The five kings have been found hidden in the cave at Makkedah."

¹⁸ Joshua said, "Roll large stones against the mouth of the cave, and assign men by it to guard them,

¹⁹ but do not stay *there* yourselves; pursue your enemies and attack them in the rear. Do not allow them to enter their cities, for the Lord your God has delivered them into your hand."

²⁰ It came about when Joshua and the sons of Israel had finished slaying them with a very great slaughter, until they were destroyed, and the survivors *who* remained of them had entered the fortified cities,

²¹ that all the people returned to the camp to Joshua at Makkedah in peace. No one uttered a word against any of the sons of Israel.

²² Then Joshua said, "Open the mouth of the cave and bring these five kings out to me from the cave."

²³ They did so, and brought these five kings out to him from the cave: the king of Jerusalem, the king of Hebron, the king of Jarmuth, the king of Lachish, *and* the king of Eglon.

²⁴ When they brought these kings out to Joshua, Joshua called for all the men of Israel, and said to the chiefs of the men of war who had gone with him, "Come near, put your feet on the necks of these kings." So they came near and put their feet on their necks.

²⁵ Joshua then said to them, "Do not fear or be dismayed! Be strong and courageous, for thus the Lord will do to all your enemies with whom you fight."

Joshua and all the warriors did not get distracted by the five kings. They tried to hide, but the Lord revealed them to Joshua and he said to seal up the cave and continue to advance. They did not get distracted from their ultimate mission. They not only conquered the kings but they went to each of their cities and took all the spoils from those cities. This means that all the spoils and inheritance that God had for them in the cities bound by the unrighteous kings was redeemed by the righteous. This is a picture of you overcoming any assault by these kings personally and then you are going to get your family, your city, and your nation out from under their control.

This is where we remain in the new land of promise and success. The sustained momentum of Joshua and Israel after this battle was exponential after they overcame these five kings. They passed the last test and so will we! When we learn how to conquer this in our hour the harvest will be substantial.

If you are facing the unholy alliance in your life humble yourself and ask the Lord to reveal how it is working against you. When you think you are healthy and moving out of the wilderness is when the enemy is actually going to try using your spiritual weapons against you. Guard against falling into this trap after getting out of the wilderness. This will ultimately destroy your life if you don't get free. Repent and ask God to free you from this snare. Give up control so God can be in control! Let go of the things you cannot hold back and allow God to break out in your life. Admit to others you are wrong without justifying your cause. This act of humility will allow God to lift you up beyond the grasps of this self righteous principality. Be willing to have true peace at the bottom rather than fighting for your right to be at the top. God will promote you in His due season.

When we are battling this spirit in the unseen realms on behalf of others we must use the power of prophetic declaration. Begin to decree out loud that the righteous seeds are going to spring forth with righteous fruit. Call in the harvest of righteousness that God ordained before that person was ever born. God created them with redemptive gifts and traits for redemptive purposes. Call them forth and wear the enemy down with your perseverance. Refuse to be silent until the harvest of righteousness comes forth!

We need to battle against this unholy alliance forming in our nation which has been stopping America from aligning with God. Our country was birthed in righteous seeds. We have a righteous destiny. We have a righteous inheritance yet to be possessed. Our season cannot end in failure and fatigue. We declare that every unfulfilled promise of God in this nation will come to fruition. We grasp the missed mantles of righteousness from the past and declare that they will be embraced and experienced in our generation. We call forth every blessing God intended for our nation that has been missed because of Adoni-zedek and we say these blessings will be experienced!

The Triumphant Declaration

I bless the church of the Living God in America and declare that you will not be destroyed by legalism and poverty. Every curse whispered must be silenced and we will shout forth the praises of the Most High God and release His presence into all the earth. We bless the families of America and say you will give life to your children and not death. You will know unity because God has joined you together and no man or spirit will tear our families asunder. We call forth the fruit of the righteous seeds in our elected officials and government. These seeds will not be corrupted and the godly harvest will not be robbed. We bless the work of God in these individuals to come to life and submission to the Lord of Lords and King of all Kings. We declare that the education system of America will once again reveal the wisdom of God. We break every curse through the passage of law that has bound our schools in death and drug abuse. We bless our children to know the Lord, fear the Lord and to live a long life. We declare that the entertainment and the arts will shine forth with the glory of God. We break the neck of compromise and rebellion. We say that the most glorious light has yet to shine through the arts in this nation. We declare that the media of this land will line up with righteousness and communicate good news. We break the curse of control and deception of this land and say we are free. We bless every righteous seed of invention and innovation God placed in our land, people and nation. We say spring up and live in this glorious hour. We call for the resources of our nation to prosper and multiply. Let the hidden wealth be discovered by the righteous and the abundance of minerals, gold and silver once more be found. Let the wealthiest businesses be based upon the ways of God and we remove all stumbling blocks of greed and mammon from the midst of our markets. We declare that the call of God upon America to make disciples of the entire nation will be fulfilled in this hour. We will not make disciples of capitalism; we will make them disciples of Jesus.

Did you feel the presence and power of God released when you read that prayer? Think what can happen when we make these kinds of decrees about our nation every day in every city! We are going to drive the enemy out of our land and we are going to possess our inheritance.

Now do the same thing for yourself and all the members of your family. Make decrees that every godly promise and calling upon your life and your family will bear fruit in this season. Declare that any seeds that have been taken hostage to be released and redeemed. Call your children home to God's kingdom by blessing the righteous seeds inside of them to come to life. Break the power of addictions in your loved ones by speaking the power of God's word and design for their destiny to be fulfilled. This is how we will continue gaining momentum.

Step forward right now into your righteous destiny. You have seeds that God planted in you before you were born. They must come to life when you fight for them to be sanctified for God's true purpose. Say out loud, I am righteous and I have peace! I am submitted to Jesus and this submission protects me. I will not be harmed by those in authority in my life; I will prosper and see fruit that I have never seen before because I am safe in my place of submission! I am moving out of my crisis! I have heard my word from God. I will move out of the wilderness. I will unite with the priests who carry God's manifest presence. I will move into the River of God. I will reap a harvest of righteousness. I will overcome all the enemies that are standing in my gate. I will praise my God in my gate. I will enter my new field. I will harvest every promise God has spoken over me in my new season. I have inherited a blessing and I am going to be a blessing. I am not alone, I am not confused.

Thank you Jesus for making me a part of your triumphant reserve!

NOTES

NOTES

MINISTRY CONTACT INFORMATION

Skyway Church
14900 West Van Buren Street
Goodyear, AZ 85338

623-935-4858
www.SkywayChurch.com